QUAKER OAT BRAN

HOT CEREAL ™

Introduction

We are a country of diet-conscious people. Motivated by a desire for total fitness, many of us are taking a closer look at what we are eating each day. And in understanding the importance of what a healthy diet should consist of, oat bran has become one of many important factors in a cholesterol reducing diet.

The dietary importance of nutritious foods, such as oat bran, is supported by the U.S. Surgeon General's recent report on nutrition and health. It states that by decreasing the amount of fat and cholesterol and increasing the consumption of grains, such as oats, cereals, vegetables and fruits in our diets, we can reduce our risk of obesity, some types of cancer and coronary heart disease. Such a diet not only tends to be lower in fat and cholesterol, but also tends to be higher in dietary fiber.

With this heightened awareness of oat bran as an important source of nutrition, people are actively seeking new ways to incorporate it into their diets. Until now, however, the means of getting oat bran into a daily diet plan has been very limited. All too often, the obvious choice for getting a substantial amount into a fat-modified diet has been through hot cereal or muffins. The Quaker Oats Company has responded to this dilemma with The Quaker Oat Bran Cookbook, a remarkable collection of delicious and healthful oat bran recipes for all meal occasions.

This book is more than just a selection of health-conscious recipes, however; it may also help in planning a healthy diet. If you're trying to reduce your blood cholesterol, Quaker Oat Bran hot cereal can play an important role in your dietary plan. In response to the growing need for diet modification to defend against specific health risks, Quaker has created this cookbook for you.

Quaker Oat Bran hot cereal is 100 percent oat bran from the outer portions of the whole oat cereal; it's the oat bran cereal which has been repeatedly and clinically tested at major leading universities, such as the University of Kentucky and Northwestern University Medical School. These tests have shown that oat bran, when used as part of a fat-modified diet, can help to reduce cholesterol levels in your blood.

The variety of great-tasting recipes in this cookbook shows you how to incorporate Quaker Oat Bran hot cereal into your diet throughout the day. These outstanding recipes have been developed in the Quaker Kitchens and meet healthful guidelines (for a description of these guidelines, see page 8). You can now enjoy delicious strawberry shortcake or vegetable pizza while adding oat bran to your diet. With the versatile recipes that follow, we hope to dispel any misconception that oat bran is just for breakfast. Oat bran never tasted better!

When it comes to oat bran, we're proud to be the expert. And, we're pleased to respond to your specific dietary needs with this series of healthy and delicious oat bran recipes.

Oat Bran, Answers to Your Questions

For many years, The Quaker Oats Company has sponsored oat research related to cholesterol reduction. And now we are pleased to take one more step in the effort towards better health by developing a variety of ways to incorporate oat bran into a fat-modified diet. The following information will provide you with important information on the basic principles of oat bran.

Oat Bran: The Definition

Oat bran is derived from the outer layers of the hulled oat kernel. The process involves grinding and sieving the kernel to produce two fractions; the coarse fraction is oat bran. The fine fraction is fine oat flour, which is used in other food products.

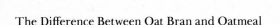

Inside Every Whole Grain Oat

The Bran is the outer covering of the grain. It is a source of valuable nutrients and one of nature's best sources of soluble fiber.

The Endosperm is the storehouse of protein and carbohydrate. It's the source of energy found in the whole grain oat.

The Germ is a source of vitamins and protein.

Bran

Endosperm

Germ

The Difference Between Oat Bran and Oatmeal

Oat bran is the outermost part of the whole oat kernel; in fact, approximately ⅓ of the whole oat kernel is oat bran. Both oat bran and oatmeal first have the inedible hull removed during processing. To make oat bran, Quaker then grinds and sieves the whole oat flour to separate out the bran portion. For oatmeal (also called rolled oats), Quaker simply flattens the hulled oats between rollers which leaves the bran portion on the oat kernel. In short, oatmeal is the whole grain, but oat bran is the outer portion of the grain.

Oat Bran and Its Role in Cholesterol Reduction

No one really knows for sure how oat bran works to reduce blood cholesterol. Scientists believe it is the type of soluble fiber in oats—called beta glucan—

that is responsible. Wheat and corn do not contain significant amounts of beta glucan, but are very good sources of insoluble fiber, which promotes regularity. Both soluble and insoluble fibers are important parts of a healthy diet.

Fiber: There are two basic classifications of dietary fiber—soluble and insoluble. Foods may contain both types of fiber, but some foods are better sources of one type of fiber than the other. Oats are an excellent source of cholesterol-reducing soluble fiber. Whole wheat products are a primary source of insoluble fiber which help to prevent constipation. Both types of fiber are important to a healthy diet, but generally only soluble fiber helps to reduce cholesterol.

Soluble Fiber: Various types of soluble fiber include hemicellulose, pectin, gums (including beta glucan) and mucilage. Not all soluble fiber has been shown to reduce blood cholesterol, however. The soluble fiber found in oat bran—gum or beta glucan—has been found to reduce blood cholesterol. Be aware of this distinction. Potatoes, for example, are billed as being high in soluble fiber. However, neither potatoes nor the fiber found in potatoes has been shown to reduce cholesterol.

Quaker Oat Bran, The Gold Standard

Quaker Oat Bran hot cereal is the first, nationally distributed, 100% oat bran with no fat, sugar or sodium added.

Research Supporting Oat Bran's Cholesterol Reduction Claim

Significant research studies have been conducted with Quaker Oat Bran hot cereal for over 10 years. It is the only oat bran product which has undergone such extensive testing. These tests have consistently and repeatedly shown that oat bran can help to reduce cholesterol when eaten daily as part of a fat-modified diet. As a result of this extensive research initiative, 100% pure Quaker Oat Bran hot cereal has earned the mark of excellence.

The series of studies demonstrating that Quaker Oat Bran hot cereal can help to reduce cholesterol, when eaten daily as part of a low fat, low cholesterol diet, have also suggested that it is the water soluble fiber found in oat products that accounts for the cholesterol reduction.

In these studies, the degree of cholesterol reduction ranged from modest to substantial depending on the individual's initial blood cholesterol level and the amount of oat product consumed. A study conducted by Northwestern University Medical School, for example, revealed an 8% reduction of blood cholesterol when a modest two ounces of oat bran were added to a fat-modified diet. Approximately one third of that reduction is attributable to the oat bran.

Overall, this long-term research initiative, supported by The Quaker Oats Company, helps demonstrate the cholesterol-reducing benefits of oat bran. And, the resulting good news is that individuals who eat oat products, along with a fat-modified diet, could benefit in the long term.

Cholesterol and Your Heart

More than half of all adult Americans have blood cholesterol levels that are higher than desirable. In fact, high blood cholesterol level is one of the primary risk factors of coronary heart disease. And coronary heart disease is blamed for nearly one quarter of all deaths in this country. It is our number one killer.

There is good news however. Most people can reduce their cholesterol level by eating foods low in saturated fat and cholesterol. In fact, the majority of the people with high blood cholesterol can lower it by modifying their diet. Research shows that oat bran, eaten as part of a fat-modified diet, can help reduce cholesterol beyond levels achieved through a fat-modified diet alone.

In order to realize the total benefits of oat bran and the relationship of cholesterol to your health however, it is important that you understand several basic principles.

Cholesterol: The Definition

Cholesterol is a soft, waxy substance present in all parts of the body. It is manufactured by the body and is present in some foods.

Blood cholesterol: Cholesterol carried in your blood that is manufactured by your liver *and* absorbed from the food you eat. A high level of blood cholesterol may lead to coronary heart disease.

Dietary cholesterol: Cholesterol that is in the food you eat. It is found in foods of animal origin. Red meat, poultry, fish, cheese, eggs and ice cream are examples of foods that contain dietary cholesterol. Cholesterol is not found in any fruit, vegetable or grain. Dietary cholesterol tends to raise blood cholesterol levels.

Dietary saturated fat, like dietary cholesterol, also raises blood cholesterol. Because saturated fat raises blood cholesterol, it has become an important consideration among cholesterol-conscious consumers. Many foods high in dietary cholesterol are also high in dietary saturated fat.

Saturated Fat and Its Contribution to Elevated Blood Cholesterol

Saturated fat is found primarily in animal products such as meat, poultry, fish, cheese, whole milk and cream. A few vegetable fats—coconut oil, palm kernel and palm oil—are also high in saturated fat. Saturated fat seems to raise blood cholesterol more than anything else in the diet and should be limited in daily menu planning.

The Role of "HDL" and "LDL" in the Cholesterol Story

High Density and Low Density lipoproteins, found in the blood, play an important role in determining your risk of heart disease. Lipoproteins are protein-coated packages that carry fat and cholesterol through the blood. Lipoproteins are classified according to their density.

High density lipoproteins (HDL): Lipoproteins that carry cholesterol away from body cells and tissues to the liver for excretion from the body. Low levels of HDL are associated with an increased risk of coronary heart disease. Therefore, the higher the HDL level, the better.

Low density lipoproteins (LDL): Lipoproteins that contain the largest amount of cholesterol in the blood. LDL is responsible for depositing cholesterol in the artery walls. High levels of LDL are associated with an increased risk of coronary heart disease. Therefore, the lower the LDL level, the better.

Primary Risk of Elevated Blood Cholesterol

High blood cholesterol is a primary risk factor for coronary heart disease. And most coronary heart disease is caused by atherosclerosis, which occurs when cholesterol and fat build up in the arteries that supply blood to the heart. Lowering blood cholesterol will slow fatty buildup in artery walls and reduce the risk of heart attack.

Be sure to have your cholesterol checked. It is important to determine what your cholesterol level is and to take steps to reduce it if it is too high.

Lowering Blood Cholesterol Levels

A diet low in saturated fat and cholesterol is recommended for treating high blood cholesterol. For most individuals, a diet low in saturated fat and cholesterol is the key to reducing high blood cholesterol. For this group of diet modifiers, Quaker Oat Bran hot cereal is important news. It can actually help to bring your cholesterol level down when used as part of a sensible diet. Because Quaker Oat Bran hot cereal can be incorporated into a variety of recipes, it is an easy way to assist in cholesterol reduction.

Reducing Your Cholesterol Level Through Diet

As illustrated in the preceding section, high blood cholesterol is a major risk to sustained good health. And proper diet is a critical step in the treatment of high blood cholesterol. In addition to helping you to reduce your cholesterol, a diet low in saturated fat and cholesterol also helps to promote weight reduction and maintenance, another important element of total fitness.

Changing your eating habits takes time. Adapting to a dietary plan, with any long-term adherence, means a complete lifestyle change. Begin adapting these dietary changes to your daily regimen gradually. Check with your doctor or registered dietitian as you begin outlining your dietary plan.

You may want to use oat bran as one important part of your diet modification. With the assistance of this cookbook, you can build complete menu plans which include the regular addition of oat bran into your diet.

To begin, review your overall eating patterns carefully. A successful attempt at diet modification requires shopping smart, preparing some foods differently, altering your choices at restaurants and consuming more foods high in complex carbohydrates and fiber and fewer foods high in saturated fat and cholesterol.

Fat-Modified Diet: The Definition

A fat-modified diet is a diet that is lower in fat than the typical American diet. Simply speaking, a fat-modified diet means cutting back on those foods high in fat and cholesterol. When eating less fat, make sure to eat less saturated fat. That's important because the best way to reduce your blood cholesterol is to reduce the amount of saturated fat that you eat.

Fat, carbohydrate and protein make up most of our daily caloric intake. The average American diet provides approximately 37% of calories from fat, 47% from carbohydrate and 16% from protein. When following a fat-modified diet, ideally your percentage of calories from saturated fat should decrease while calories from complex carbohydrates should increase. The following are important dietary guidelines, by the National Cholesterol Education Program, for lowering high blood cholesterol.

Dietary Guidelines

· Eat less than 30% of your total daily calories from fat.

· Less than 10% of your total daily calories should come from saturated fat. No more than 10% of your calories should come from polyunsaturated fat and 10% to 15% of your calories should come from monounsaturated fat.

· Eat less than 300 mg of cholesterol each day.

· Eat 50% to 60% of your total daily calories from carbohydrates.

· Adjust your caloric intake to achieve a desirable weight.

Foods high in soluble fiber can also provide a significant dietary benefit. Quaker Oat Bran hot cereal, for example, provides an effective source of soluble fiber and it is the oat bran that has undergone repeated testing. These tests have shown that oat bran can help reduce blood cholesterol levels when eaten daily as part of a fat-modified diet.

Calculating the Percentage of Calories from Fat

The following equation will help you to determine your calories from fat. Calculate the amount of fat you eat by referring to food package labels.

Total fat (grams) $\times$ 9 = Total Fat Calories

$$\frac{\text{Total fat calories}}{\text{Total calories}} \times 100 = \% \text{ calories from fat}$$

Changing the way you prepare a variety of foods can help to reduce the amount of total and saturated fats. Below are a series of low-fat cooking tips which can help you prepare foods that are good for your heart.

- When preparing poultry, meat or fish, trim off all visible fat. Remove the skin from poultry before cooking.
- Broil, roast, poach or bake meats, poultry or fish rather than frying them.
- When basting foods, use fat-free ingredients like tomato sauce, or lemon or lime juice instead of fatty drippings.
- Select tuna or other fish packed in water rather than oil.

Guide to Using this Book Effectively

The Quaker Oat Bran Cookbook is proof that Quaker Oat Bran is more than just a breakfast cereal. The series of recipes that follow demonstrate how you can incorporate oat bran into your diet through delicious breads, entrees, side dishes, desserts, snacks and appetizers, in addition to breakfast. Each of the recipes were carefully prepared by the Quaker Kitchens with the health-conscious and serious diet-modifying consumer in mind.

Great care has been taken with each recipe to maximize the amount of oat bran per serving and to substitute ingredients that are high in fat and cholesterol with low-fat alternatives. Special attention has also been paid to each recipe to ensure that the rich flavor and texture of the prepared food is not lost. For example, cocoa has been substituted for high-fat chocolate in several dessert recipes. For the chocolate-lover who is also modifying his diet, he can still have the rich taste of chocolate without the unnecessary fat. Below are several other ingredient substitutes which help to achieve the foods' natural flavors while reducing cholesterol, sodium and fat.

Ingredient	Substitute Used
Whole eggs	Egg whites
Butter	Vegetable oil/margarine
Whole/2% milk	Skim milk
Cheeses	Low fat cheeses
Vegetable/tomato juice	Low sodium juices
Sour cream	Plain low fat yogurt
Ground beef	Extra lean ground beef
Whipped cream	Dessert topping mix prepared with skim milk

In order to help you incorporate these recipes into your diet, the Quaker Kitchens have provided nutrition information at the end of each recipe. The Quaker Kitchens have also developed these recipes to fit generally within the daily dietary guidelines of a fat-modified diet.

Because dietary guidelines are established by overall daily food intake, it is difficult to determine recommended nutrient levels for specific recipes without knowing an individual's complete daily menu plan. Quaker nutritionists have responded by designing specific recipe guidelines which help ensure that all recipes included in the cookbook can fit into an overall healthy dietary plan. All of the following recipes are designed to fit into a total fat-modified dietary plan.

The following chart lists the average nutrient levels for all of the recipes. For example, the average milligrams of cholesterol for all recipes is 9 mg. In fact, no individual recipe exceeds 120 mg per serving. The average calories from fat is 26%, with 45% calories from fat at the high end. Please note, when incorporating the limited number of individual recipes which are higher in the percentage of calories from fat, plan your total daily intake carefully. Make sure that your other food choices for that day are low in fat so that your total daily calories from fat remains in line. Overall, review your daily food choices carefully to ensure the proper diet balance. Specific nutrient profiles are also included with each individual recipe to help in the planning process. This information reflects a good estimate of the nutrient values. In most recipes the numbers have been rounded. These nutritionals reflect only the basic recipe. Optional ingredients were not included in calculating the nutritionals. If you choose to incorporate any of the recipe tip suggestions, or optional ingredients, those food choices should be taken into consideration as part of your daily dietary intake.

When developing your daily dietary plan, review the nutritional information carefully. You may wish to contact your physician or registered dietitian to help you develop a meal plan that specifically fits your needs.

Nutritional Recipe Content	**Average for Total Recipes**
· % Calories from fat	26%
· Cholesterol	9 mg
· Sodium	125 mg
· Dietary Fiber	3 g

The oat bran content of each recipe ranges from 4 grams to 28 grams per serving. The daily amount of oat bran targeted in the Northwestern University study for cholesterol reduction, when used as part of a fat-modified diet, was 2 ounces or 56 grams. Compare this amount against the oat bran content of each recipe to develop a menu incorporating the comparable levels of oat bran. For example, each of the following recipe combinations, when eaten in one day, will provide you with 2 ounces of oat bran per day:

· Spiced Oat Bran Cereal and 2 Blueberry Yogurt Muffins, or

· Raisin 'n Orange Oat Bran Cereal and 1 slice Vegetable Pizza with Oat Bran Crust and 1 serving Very Strawberry Shortcake, or

· Fruit Smoothie Shake and 1 Giant Raisin Oat Cookie and 1 serving Zucchini Bake.

Whether you are interested in general health and fitness or diet modification, The Quaker Oat Bran Cookbook can assist you with your individual dietary needs.

Breakfast, for a healthy start

Start the day right with these great-tasting, healthful oat bran recipes. For a leisurely Sunday brunch try Apple Raisin Crepes or hearty Oat Bran Pancakes. When you're off to a quick weekday start, whip up an icy Fruit Smoothie Shake or brown bag a Cranberry Banana Muffin for breakfast on the go.

Pictured here are Oat Bran 'n Ginger Waffles. See page 12 for recipe.

Oat Bran 'n Ginger Waffles

Enjoy the sweet aroma of these waffles with the healthful benefit of oat bran. Top with fresh fruit.

2 egg whites
1 cup Quaker Oat Bran hot cereal, uncooked
1 cup all-purpose flour
½ cup sugar
1 teaspoon ginger
½ teaspoon cinnamon
½ teaspoon baking soda

½ teaspoon baking powder
¼ teaspoon ground cloves (optional)
¼ teaspoon salt (optional)
1 cup skim milk
3 tablespoons vegetable oil
2 tablespoons dark molasses

Heat waffle iron according to manufacturer's instructions. Beat egg whites until soft peaks form; set aside. Combine oat bran, flour, sugar, ginger, cinnamon, baking soda, baking powder, cloves and salt; mix well. Whisk milk, oil and molasses until well blended. Add to dry ingredients, mixing just until moistened. Do not overmix. Fold egg whites into batter. Pour about 1 cup batter onto surface of grid. Close the lid; bake until steam no longer escapes from sides of the iron and waffles are deep golden brown. Serve with fruit or Aunt Jemima Lite or ButterLite Syrup, if desired.   *Makes 6 servings*

Nutrition information: Each serving (2 waffles)

Calories 290	Fat 8 g	**Oat Bran 14 g**
Protein 7 g	polyunsaturated 4 g	Dietary Fiber 3 g
Carbohydrate 47 g	monounsaturated 2 g	Sodium 150 mg
	saturated 1 g	Cholesterol 0 mg

Percentage of calories from fat: 26%
Diabetic exchanges: 2 Starch/Bread; 1½ Fat; 1 Fruit

Spiced Oat Bran Cereal

Savor the aroma of traditional oat bran blended with the rich flavors of cinnamon and nutmeg. Prepare in the microwave for a quick breakfast.

⅔ cup skim milk
⅓ cup water
⅓ cup Quaker Oat Bran hot
    cereal, uncooked

¼ teaspoon vanilla
⅛ teaspoon cinnamon
Dash of nutmeg
Dash of salt (optional)

In small saucepan, combine all ingredients. Bring to a boil; reduce heat. Cook 1 minute, stirring occasionally. Let stand until thickened. Serve with skim milk and sugar or sugar substitute, if desired.

Makes 1 serving

MICROWAVE DIRECTIONS: In 2-cup microwaveable bowl, combine all ingredients. Microwave at HIGH 2 minutes to 2 minutes 30 seconds, or until cereal begins to thicken; stir. Serve with skim milk and sugar or sugar substitute, if desired.

Nutrition information: Each serving (1 cup)

Calories 170	Fat 3 g	**Oat Bran 28 g**
Protein 11 g	polyunsaturated 1 g	Dietary Fiber 4 g
Carbohydrate 25 g	monounsaturated 1 g	Sodium 85 mg
	saturated 1 g	Cholesterol 5 mg

Percentage of calories from fat: 15%
Diabetic exchanges: 1½ Starch/Bread; ½ Milk

--- ♥ ♥ ♥ ---

Sprinkle uncooked Quaker Oat Bran hot cereal or sweet oat bran toppings on pages 89 and 92 over oatmeal or cold cereals for added nutrition.

Oat Bran Pancakes

For a weekend treat, serve these light and fluffy breakfast cakes. Make a second batch and freeze for a quick weekday breakfast. Serve with yogurt or fruit for an extra delicious touch.

1 cup Quaker Oat Bran hot cereal, uncooked	**2 teaspoons baking powder**
½ cup all-purpose flour	**1 cup skim milk**
1 to 2 teaspoons sugar	**1 tablespoon vegetable oil**
	1 egg white, slightly beaten

Heat griddle over medium-high heat (375°F electric griddle); lightly spray with vegetable oil cooking spray or oil lightly. Combine oat bran, flour, sugar and baking powder. Add combined milk, oil and egg white; mix well.* Pour scant ¼ cup batter for each pancake onto prepared griddle. Turn pancakes when tops are covered with bubbles and edges look cooked. Turn only once. Serve with Aunt Jemima Lite or ButterLite syrup or low fat yogurt and fresh fruit, if desired. *Makes 4 servings*

*Batter will thicken upon standing. For best results, cook pancakes immediately after mixing.

Variation: For Fruit Pancakes, fold in 1 cup chopped fruit just before cooking.

Tips

To keep pancakes warm: Heat oven to 250°F. Place pancakes in single layer on ungreased cookie sheet; cover tightly with foil. Keep in warm oven up to 10 minutes.

To freeze pancakes: Stack with waxed paper between each pancake. Wrap securely in foil or place in freezer bag. Seal, label and freeze.

To reheat frozen pancakes: Unwrap 3 pancakes; wrap in paper towel. Microwave at HIGH about 1 minute 30 seconds or until warm.

Nutrition information: Each serving (3 pancakes)

Calories 200	Fat 6 g	**Oat Bran 21 g**
Protein 9 g	polyunsaturated 3 g	Dietary Fiber 3 g
Carbohydrate 29 g	monounsaturated 1 g	Sodium 260 mg
	saturated 1 g	Cholesterol 0 mg

Percentage of calories from fat: 25%
Diabetic exchanges: 2 Starch/Bread; 1 Fat

Double Oat Muffins

The combination of oats and oat bran create a healthful grain muffin perfect for breakfast or as a snack. Prepare in the microwave for fresh, hot muffins anytime.

2 cups Quaker Oat Bran hot cereal, uncooked
⅓ cup firmly packed brown sugar
¼ cup all-purpose flour
2 teaspoons baking powder
¼ teaspoon salt (optional)
¼ teaspoon nutmeg (optional)

1 cup skim milk
2 egg whites, slightly beaten
3 tablespoons vegetable oil
1½ teaspoons vanilla
¼ cup Quaker Oats (quick or old fashioned, uncooked)
1 tablespoon firmly packed brown sugar

Heat oven to 400°F. Line 12 medium muffin cups with paper baking cups. Combine oat bran, ⅓ cup brown sugar, flour, baking powder, salt and nutmeg. Add combined milk, egg whites, oil and vanilla, mixing just until moistened. Fill muffin cups almost full. Combine oats and remaining 1 tablespoon brown sugar; sprinkle evenly over batter. Bake 20 to 22 minutes or until golden brown.   *Makes 1 dozen*

MICROWAVE DIRECTIONS: Line 6 microwaveable muffin cups with double paper baking cups. Combine oat bran, ⅓ cup brown sugar, flour, baking powder, salt and nutmeg. Add combined milk, egg whites, oil and vanilla, mixing just until moistened. Fill muffin cups almost full. Combine oats and remaining 1 tablespoon brown sugar; sprinkle evenly over batter. Microwave at HIGH 2 minutes 30 seconds to 3 minutes or until wooden pick inserted in center comes out clean. Remove from pan; cool 5 minutes before serving. Line muffin cups with additional double paper baking cups. Repeat procedure with remaining batter.

Tips
To freeze muffins: Wrap securely in foil or place in freezer bag. Seal, label and freeze.

To reheat frozen muffins: Unwrap muffins. Microwave at HIGH about 30 seconds per muffin.

Nutrition information: Each serving (1 muffin)

Calories 140	Fat 5 g	**Oat Bran 16 g**
Protein 5 g	polyunsaturated 2 g	Dietary Fiber 2 g
Carbohydrate 19 g	monounsaturated 1 g	Sodium 90 mg
	saturated 0 g	Cholesterol 0 mg

Percentage of calories from fat: 31%
Diabetic exchanges: 1 Starch/Bread; 1 Fat; ½ Fruit

Double Oat Muffins

Raisin 'n Orange Oat Bran Cereal

Start your day with this delicious hot breakfast, sweetened naturally with raisins and orange juice. Try microwave preparation for a quick start.

½ cup orange juice
½ cup water
⅓ cup Quaker Oat Bran hot
    cereal, uncooked

1 tablespoon raisins
Dash of cinnamon
Dash of salt (optional)

In small saucepan, combine all ingredients. Bring to a boil; reduce heat. Cook 1 minute, stirring occasionally. Let stand until thickened. Serve with skim milk and sugar or sugar substitute, if desired.

Makes 1 serving

MICROWAVE DIRECTIONS: In 2-cup microwaveable bowl, combine all ingredients. Microwave at HIGH 2 minutes to 2 minutes 30 seconds, or until cereal begins to thicken; stir. Serve with skim milk and sugar or sugar substitute, if desired.

Nutrition information: Each serving (1 cup)

Calories 190	Fat 3 g	Oat Bran 28 g
Protein 7 g	polyunsaturated 1 g	Dietary Fiber 5 g
Carbohydrate 37 g	monounsaturated 1 g	Sodium 5 mg
	saturated 0 g	Cholesterol 0 mg

Percentage of calories from fat: 12%
Diabetic exchanges: 1½ Starch/Bread; 1 Fruit

♥   ♥   ♥

Sprinkle 1 to 2 teaspoons uncooked Quaker Oat Bran hot cereal or Sugar 'n Spice Topping on page 89 over each half of broiled or baked grapefruit.

Raisin 'n Orange Oat Bran Cereal

Cranberry Banana Muffins

Tart cranberries and ripened, sweet bananas provide an extra twist to the traditional oat bran muffin. Freeze and reheat in the microwave for fresh, hot baked muffins anytime.

2 cups Quaker Oat Bran hot cereal, uncooked	**½ cup finely chopped cranberries**
½ cup firmly packed brown sugar	**⅔ cup cranberry juice cocktail**
¼ cup all-purpose flour	**½ cup mashed ripe banana (about 1 medium)**
2 teaspoons baking powder	**2 egg whites, slightly beaten**
½ teaspoon salt (optional)	**3 tablespoons vegetable oil**
½ teaspoon cinnamon	

Heat oven to 400°F. Line 12 medium muffin cups with paper baking cups. Combine oat bran, brown sugar, flour, baking powder, salt and cinnamon. Gently stir in cranberries. Add combined cranberry juice, banana, egg whites and oil, mixing just until moistened. Fill muffin cups almost full. Bake 20 to 22 minutes or until golden brown.

Makes 1 dozen

Tips

To freeze muffins: Wrap securely in foil or place in freezer bag. Seal, label and freeze.

To reheat frozen muffins: Unwrap muffins. Microwave at HIGH about 30 seconds per muffin.

Nutrition information: Each serving (1 muffin)

Calories 150	Fat 5 g	**Oat Bran 14 g**
Protein 4 g	polyunsaturated 2 g	Dietary Fiber 2 g
Carbohydrate 24 g	monounsaturated 2 g	Sodium 85 mg
	saturated 0 g	Cholesterol 0 mg

Percentage of calories from fat: 28%
Diabetic exchanges: 1 Starch / Bread; 1 Fat; ½ Fruit

♥   ♥   ♥

Replace all of the flour in your favorite muffin recipe with oat bran. For a lighter, more cake-like muffin, add ¼ cup flour to the original recipe along with the oat bran replacement.

Swiss Oat 'n Apple Cereal

The perfect breakfast solution for a busy week. Prepare this delicious cereal ahead of time and refrigerate for use throughout the week. Serve hot or cold.

4 cups natural or chunky applesauce
1⅓ cups Quaker Oat Bran hot cereal, uncooked
1 cup Quaker Oats (quick or old fashioned, uncooked)

1 cup unsweetened apple juice
⅔ cup raisins
¼ cup sliced almonds
1 teaspoon cinnamon

Combine all ingredients; mix well. Cover; refrigerate overnight. Store in refrigerator up to 1 week. Serve cold or hot* with skim milk or low fat yogurt, if desired.   *Makes 5 servings*

*To heat one serving, place ¾ cup cereal in 2-cup microwaveable bowl. Microwave at HIGH 1 minute 30 seconds to 2 minutes or until heated through; stir.

Nutrition information: Each serving (¾ cup)

Calories 345	Fat 6 g	**Oat Bran 28 g**
Protein 9 g	polyunsaturated 2 g	Dietary Fiber 9 g
Carbohydrate 68 g	monounsaturated 2 g	Sodium 10 mg
	saturated 1 g	Cholesterol 0 mg

Percentage of calories from fat: 14%
Diabetic exchanges: 2½ Starch/Bread; 2 Fruit; ½ Fat

Oat Bran
from the Expert™

Apple Raisin Crepes

These delicious crepes are the perfect Sunday brunch entree. Also try this basic crepe recipe with a variety of other menu ideas—fill with your favorite fruits or vegetables for a tasty dessert or side dish.

¾ cup Quaker Oat Bran hot
   cereal, uncooked
1 teaspoon baking powder
1 cup skim milk
3 egg whites, slightly beaten
1 tablespoon liquid vegetable oil
   margarine
1 cup part skim ricotta cheese

1 small apple, finely chopped
⅔ cup raisins
1 tablespoon powdered sugar
½ teaspoon vanilla
⅔ cup Aunt Jemima Lite or
   ButterLite Syrup
¼ teaspoon cinnamon

Combine oat bran and baking powder; add combined milk, egg whites and margarine, mixing well. Heat 6 to 7-inch crepe pan or skillet over medium heat; lightly spray with vegetable oil cooking spray or oil lightly before making each crepe. Pour about ¼ cup batter onto hot prepared pan; immediately tilt pan to coat bottom evenly. Cook 1 to 1½ minutes or until top looks dry. Turn; cook an additional 1 minute. Stack between sheets of waxed paper.

Combine ricotta, apple, raisins, sugar and vanilla; mix well. Spoon about 2 tablespoons along less evenly browned side of each crepe. Fold or roll up sides to cover filling. Combine syrup and cinnamon; heat over medium heat about 2 minutes, stirring occasionally, or until heated through. Just before serving, pour 2 tablespoons over each crepe.

Makes 5 servings (10 crepes)

Tips

To freeze crepes: Stack with 2 layers of waxed paper between each crepe. Wrap securely in foil or place in freezer bag. Seal, label and freeze. Thaw frozen crepes at room temperature about 1 hour before filling.

To reheat frozen crepes: Unwrap 2 crepes; wrap in paper towel. Microwave at LOW to MEDIUM-LOW (30% power) about 1 minute 30 seconds or until warm.

Nutrition information: Each serving (2 crepes)

Calories 300	Fat 7 g	Oat Bran 13 g
Protein 12 g	polyunsaturated 1 g	Dietary Fiber 3 g
Carbohydrate 48 g	monounsaturated 2 g	Sodium 290 mg
	saturated 3 g	Cholesterol 15 mg

Percentage of calories from fat: 22%
Diabetic Exchanges: 2 Starch/Bread; 1 Fat; ½ Milk; ½ Medium Fat Meat

Apple Raisin Crepes

Blueberry Yogurt Muffins

Try these moist, flourless yogurt muffins sweetened with the natural taste of honey and blueberry. Pack these portable treats in your briefcase for an afternoon snack.

2 cups Quaker Oat Bran hot cereal, uncooked
¼ cup firmly packed brown sugar
2 teaspoons baking powder
1 carton (8 oz.) plain low fat yogurt

2 egg whites, slightly beaten
¼ cup skim milk
¼ cup honey
2 tablespoons vegetable oil
1 teaspoon grated lemon peel
½ cup fresh or frozen blueberries

Heat oven to 425°F. Line 12 medium muffin cups with paper baking cups. Combine oat bran, brown sugar and baking powder. Add combined yogurt, egg whites, skim milk, honey, oil and lemon peel, mixing just until moistened. Fold in blueberries. Fill muffin cups almost full. Bake 18 to 20 minutes or until golden brown.   *Makes 12 muffins*

Tips
To freeze muffins: Wrap securely in foil or place in freezer bag. Seal, label and freeze.

To reheat frozen muffins: Unwrap muffins. Microwave at HIGH about 30 seconds per muffin.

Nutrition information: Each serving (1 muffin)

Calories 130	Fat 4 g	Oat Bran 14 g
Protein 5 g	polyunsaturated 2 g	Dietary Fiber 2 g
Carbohydrate 21 g	monounsaturated 1 g	Sodium 100 mg
	saturated 1 g	Cholesterol 0 mg

Percentage of calories from fat: 25%
Diabetic exchanges: 1 Starch/Bread; ½ Fruit; ½ Fat

♥   ♥   ♥

Sprinkle ½ to 1 teaspoon uncooked Quaker Oat Bran hot cereal or sweet oat bran toppings on pages 89 and 92 over fruit shakes and smoothies on page 28 or over fruit crisps.

Healthy Oat Granola

Use this granola as a hot or cold cereal or as a crunchy topping for fruits and yogurt. Easy microwave preparation makes fresh granola possible anytime.

1⅔ cups Quaker Oat Bran hot cereal, uncooked
1 cup Quaker Oats (quick or old fashioned, uncooked)
⅓ cup instant nonfat dry milk solids
¼ cup honey
¼ cup hulled sunflower seeds
2 tablespoons vegetable oil
2 tablespoons water
1 teaspoon grated orange peel
½ teaspoon vanilla
¾ cup dried banana chips
½ cup raisins

Heat oven to 350°F. Combine oat bran, oats, dry milk solids, honey, sunflower seeds, oil, water, orange peel and vanilla; mix well. Spread in 13×9-inch baking pan. Bake 20 to 25 minutes or until golden brown, stirring once after 10 minutes. Stir in banana chips and raisins. Cool completely. Store tightly covered up to 1 week. Serve cold or hot* with skim milk or as a topping over fruit, low fat yogurt or ice milk, if desired.

Makes 5 servings

MICROWAVE DIRECTIONS: In large microwaveable bowl, combine oat bran, oats, dry milk solids, honey, sunflower seeds, oil, water, orange peel and vanilla; mix well. Microwave at HIGH 5 to 6 minutes, stirring after 3 minutes. Stir in banana chips and raisins. Spread mixture onto foil. Cool completely. Store tightly covered up to 1 week. Serve cold or hot* with skim milk or as a topping over fruit, low fat yogurt or ice milk, if desired.

*To heat 1 serving hot cereal, place 1 cup granola in 2-cup microwaveable bowl. Add ½ cup skim milk. Microwave at HIGH about 1 minute 30 seconds or until heated through; stir.

Nutrition information: Each serving (about 1 cup)

Calories 430	Fat 13 g	**Oat Bran 28 g**
Protein 13 g	polyunsaturated 7 g	Dietary Fiber 6 g
Carbohydrate 70 g	monounsaturated 3 g	Sodium 30 mg
	saturated 2 g	Cholesterol 0 mg

Percentage of calories from fat: 26%
Diabetic exchanges: 2½ Starch/Bread; 2 Fruit; 2 Fat; ¼ Milk

Healthy Oat Granola

Fruit Smoothie Shake

Made with skim milk and your favorite fruit, this shake is a healthful alternative to the traditional ice-cream-based drink. Plenty of ice is the key to this perfect cold and creamy drink.

1 cup ice cubes
1 cup skim milk
1 ripe banana, sliced, or 1 cup
   any fresh or frozen fruit*

⅓ cup Quaker Oat Bran hot
   cereal, uncooked
2 teaspoons sugar or sugar
   substitute (optional)

Place all ingredients in blender container or food processor bowl; cover. Blend or process on high speed until smooth and thick. Serve immediately.   *Makes 1 serving*

*Substitute 1 cup canned fruit in juice, well drained.

Nutrition information: Each serving (1¾ cups)

Calories 330	Fat 3 g	Oat Bran 28 g
Protein 15 g	polyunsaturated 1 g	Dietary Fiber 6 g
Carbohydrate 63 g	monounsaturated 1 g	Sodium 130 mg
	saturated 1 g	Cholesterol 5 mg

Percentage of calories from fat: 9%
Diabetic exchanges: 2 Fruit; 1½ Starch/Bread; 1 Milk

Frosty Juice Shake

For a quick and easy breakfast boost or a mid-afternoon break, prepare an icy cold juice shake. An exciting new way to get oat bran into your diet.

1 cup ice cubes
⅔ cup any flavor fruit juice
1 small ripe banana, sliced
⅓ cup Quaker Oat Bran hot
   cereal, uncooked

½ to 1 teaspoon sugar or sugar
   substitute (optional)
Dash of cinnamon

Place all ingredients in blender container or food processor bowl; cover. Blend or process on high speed until smooth and thick. Serve immediately.   *Makes 1 serving*

Nutrition information: Each serving (1¾ cups)

Calories 250	Fat 3 g	Oat Bran 28 g
Protein 6 g	polyunsaturated 1 g	Dietary Fiber 5 g
Carbohydrate 53 g	monounsaturated 1 g	Sodium 5 mg
	saturated 1 g	Cholesterol 0 mg

Percentage of calories from fat: 10%
Diabetic exchanges: 2 Fruit; 1½ Starch/Bread

Fruit Smoothie Shake (left),
Frosty Juice Shake (right)

Breads, fresh from the oven

Fresh baked breads can be a delicious part of any meal. Now, they can also be a wonderful way to introduce oat bran into your diet. Prepare a quick bread as an accompaniment to any meal or as a healthy mid-morning snack. Or, build a nutritious sandwich with a couple of slices of yeast bread.

Pictured here is Touch of Honey Bread. See page 32 for recipe.

Touch of Honey Bread

The ideal sandwich bread! Try this high rising, light loaf for sandwiches, toast or as a complement to any meal.

2½ to 3 cups all-purpose flour
  1 cup Quaker Oat Bran hot
    cereal, uncooked
  1 pkg. quick-rise yeast

½ teaspoon salt
1¼ cups water
2 tablespoons honey
2 tablespoons margarine

In large mixer bowl, combine 1 cup flour, oat bran, yeast and salt. Heat water, honey and margarine until very warm (120° to 130°F). Add to dry ingredients; beat at low speed of electric mixer until moistened. Increase speed to medium; continue beating 3 minutes. Stir in enough remaining flour to form a stiff dough.

Lightly spray bowl with vegetable oil cooking spray or oil lightly. Turn dough out onto lightly floured surface. Knead 8 to 10 minutes or until dough is smooth and elastic. Place into prepared bowl, turning once to coat surface of dough. Cover; let rise in warm place 30 minutes or until doubled in size.

Lightly spray 8×4-inch loaf pan with vegetable oil cooking spray or oil lightly. Punch down dough. Roll into 15×7-inch rectangle. Starting at narrow end, roll up dough tightly. Pinch ends and seam to seal; place seam side down in prepared pan. Cover; let rise in warm place 30 minutes or until doubled in size.

Heat oven to 375°F. Bake 35 to 40 minutes or until golden brown. Remove from pan; cool on wire rack at least 1 hour before slicing. Serve as sandwich bread, toasted or spread with jelly, jam or fruit preserves.

Makes 16 slices

Nutrition information: Each serving (¹⁄₁₆ of bread)

Calories 120	Fat 2 g	**Oat Bran 6 g**
Protein 3 g	polyunsaturated 0 g	Dietary Fiber 1 g
Carbohydrate 22 g	monounsaturated 1 g	Sodium 85 mg
	saturated 0 g	Cholesterol 0 mg

Percentage of calories from fat: 16%
Diabetic exchanges: 1½ Starch/Bread; ½ Fat

Pepper Cheese Bread

Low fat cheese combined with black pepper adds a spicy touch to this savory bread. Quick rising yeast is used for preparation shortcuts.

1 teaspoon Quaker or Aunt
   Jemima Enriched Corn Meal
2 to 2½ cups all-purpose flour
1 cup Quaker Oat Bran hot
   cereal, uncooked
2 teaspoons sugar
½ to 1 teaspoon pepper

1 pkg. quick-rise yeast
⅛ teaspoon baking soda
1 cup water
¼ cup skim milk
2 tablespoons margarine
1 cup (4 oz.) shredded low fat
   cheddar cheese

Lightly spray 8×4-inch loaf pan with vegetable oil cooking spray or oil lightly. Sprinkle sides and bottom with corn meal. In large mixer bowl, combine 1 cup flour, oat bran, sugar, pepper, yeast and baking soda. Heat water, milk and margarine until very warm (120° to 130°F). Add to dry ingredients; beat at low speed of electric mixer until moistened. Add cheese. Increase speed to medium; continue beating 3 minutes. Stir in enough remaining flour to form a stiff dough.

Turn out onto lightly floured surface. Knead 8 to 10 minutes or until dough is smooth and elastic. Roll into 15×7-inch rectangle. Starting at narrow end, roll up dough tightly. Pinch ends and seam to seal; place seam side down in prepared pan. Cover; let rise in warm place about 30 minutes or until doubled in size.

Heat oven to 375°F. Bake 30 to 35 minutes or until golden brown. Remove from pan; cool on wire rack at least 1 hour before slicing. Serve as sandwich bread or as a main-meal accompaniment.   *Makes 16 slices*

Nutrition information: Each serving (¹⁄₁₆ of loaf)

Calories 120	Fat 3 g	**Oat Bran 6 g**
Protein 5 g	polyunsaturated 0 g	Dietary Fiber 1 g
Carbohydrate 18 g	monounsaturated 1 g	Sodium 80 mg
	saturated 1 g	Cholesterol 5 mg

Percentage of calories from fat: 24%
Diabetic exchanges: 1 Starch/Bread; ½ Fat; ¼ Lean Meat

Banana Bran Loaf

Savor the flavor of an all-time favorite with the added healthful benefit of oat bran.

1 cup mashed ripe bananas (about 2 large)	⅓ cup skim milk
½ cup sugar	1¼ cups all-purpose flour
⅓ cup liquid vegetable oil margarine	1 cup Quaker Oat Bran hot cereal, uncooked
2 egg whites	2 teaspoons baking powder
	½ teaspoon baking soda

Heat oven to 350°F. Lightly spray 8×4-inch or 9×5-inch loaf pan with vegetable oil cooking spray or oil lightly. Combine bananas, sugar, margarine, egg whites and milk; mix well. Add combined flour, oat bran, baking powder and baking soda, mixing just until moistened. Pour into prepared pan. Bake 55 to 60 minutes or until wooden pick inserted in center comes out clean. Cool 10 minutes in pan; remove to wire rack. Cool completely. *Makes 16 servings*

Tips
To freeze bread slices: Layer waxed paper between each slice of bread. Wrap securely in foil or place in freezer bag. Seal, label and freeze.

To reheat bread slices: Unwrap frozen bread slices; wrap in paper towel. Microwave at HIGH about 30 seconds for each slice, or until warm.

Nutrition information: Each serving (¹⁄₁₆ of loaf)

Calories 130	Fat 4 g	**Oat Bran 5 g**
Protein 3 g	polyunsaturated 2 g	Dietary Fiber 1 g
Carbohydrate 20 g	monounsaturated 0 g	Sodium 110 mg
	saturated 1 g	Cholesterol 0 mg

Percentage of calories from fat: 30%
Diabetic exchanges: 1 Starch/Bread; ½ Fruit; ½ Fat

♥ ♥ ♥

Quick breads can be prepared by replacing up to half the flour in the original recipe with oat bran. Depending on the amount of oat bran you wish to incorporate into your daily diet, substitute any percentage of oat bran for the flour up to, but not exceeding, one half.

Banana Bran Loaf

Oats 'n Fruit Coffee Cake

This "quick" bread, with the subtle flavor of apricots, is delicious when made in the oven or microwave. Substitute dried fruits like prunes or figs for apricots.

¾ cup Quaker Oats (quick or old
    fashioned, uncooked)
2 tablespoons sugar
½ teaspoon cinnamon
2 tablespoons liquid vegetable
    oil margarine
1 cup sugar
¼ cup liquid vegetable oil
    margarine

⅔ cup skim milk
2 egg whites, slightly beaten
1 teaspoon vanilla
1 cup whole wheat flour
½ cup Quaker Oat Bran hot
    cereal, uncooked
1 teaspoon baking powder
½ cup chopped dried apricots,
    raisins, dates, prunes or figs

Combine oats, 2 tablespoons sugar and cinnamon. Stir in 2 tablespoons margarine; mix well. Set aside.

Heat oven to 350°F. Lightly spray 8 or 9-inch square baking pan with vegetable oil cooking spray or oil lightly. Beat 1 cup sugar and ¼ cup margarine until well blended. Add combined milk, egg whites and vanilla; mix well. Add combined whole wheat flour, oat bran and baking powder, mixing until well blended. Spread into prepared pan; sprinkle evenly with apricots. Top with reserved oat mixture to cover apricots. Bake 35 to 40 minutes or until wooden pick inserted in center comes out clean. Cool completely on wire rack. Wrap securely; store at room temperature.

Makes 9 servings

MICROWAVE DIRECTIONS: Combine oats, 2 tablespoons sugar and cinnamon. Stir in 2 tablespoons margarine; mix well. Set aside.

Beat 1 cup sugar and ¼ cup margarine until well blended. Add combined milk, egg whites and vanilla; mix well. Add combined whole wheat flour, oat bran and baking powder, mixing until well blended. Spread into ungreased 8-inch square microwaveable dish; sprinkle evenly with apricots. Top with reserved oat mixture to cover apricots. Microwave at MEDIUM-LOW to MEDIUM (50% power) 6 minutes, rotating dish after 3 minutes. Microwave at HIGH 4 to 6 minutes or until center springs back when lightly touched. Cool completely. Wrap securely; store at room temperature.

Nutrition information: Each serving (⅑ of cake)

Calories 280	Fat 8 g	**Oat Bran 7 g**
Protein 5 g	polyunsaturated 7 g	Dietary Fiber 4 g
Carbohydrate 47 g	monounsaturated 0 g	Sodium 125 mg
	saturated 1 g	Cholesterol 0 mg

Percentage of calories from fat: 27%
Diabetic exchanges: 2 Starch/Bread; 1½ Fat; 1 Fruit

Oats 'n Fruit Coffee Cake

Oat 'n Carrot Loaf

The rich color and flavor of carrots combined with oat bran creates a light bread with a rich brown crust.

2⅓ to 2⅔ cups all-purpose flour
1 cup Quaker Oat Bran hot
   cereal, uncooked
¼ cup firmly packed brown
   sugar
1 pkg. quick-rise yeast
½ teaspoon salt

⅓ cup skim milk
¼ cup water
¼ cup (½ stick) margarine
1 cup shredded carrots (about
   3 medium)
2 egg whites

In large mixer bowl, combine 1 cup flour, oat bran, brown sugar, yeast and salt. Heat milk, water and margarine until very warm (120° to 130°F). Add to dry ingredients; beat at low speed of electric mixer until moistened. Add carrots and egg whites. Increase speed to medium; continue beating 3 minutes. Stir in enough remaining flour to form a stiff dough.

Lightly spray large bowl with vegetable oil cooking spray or oil lightly. Turn dough out onto lightly floured surface. Knead 8 to 10 minutes or until dough is smooth and elastic. Place in prepared bowl, turning once to coat surface of dough. Cover; let rise in warm place about 1 hour or until doubled in size.

Lightly spray 8×4-inch loaf pan with vegetable oil cooking spray or oil lightly. Punch down dough. Roll into 15×7-inch rectangle. Starting at narrow end, roll up dough tightly. Pinch ends and seam to seal; place seam side down in prepared pan. Cover; let rise in warm place 45 minutes or until doubled in size.

Heat oven to 375°F. Bake 25 to 30 minutes or until golden brown. Remove from pan; cool on wire rack at least 1 hour before slicing. Serve toasted and topped with low fat cheese or spread with jelly, jam or fruit preserves.   *Makes 16 slices*

Nutrition information: Each serving (¹⁄₁₆ of loaf)

Calories 140	Fat 3 g	**Oat Bran 6 g**
Protein 4 g	polyunsaturated 1 g	Dietary Fiber 2 g
Carbohydrate 22 g	monounsaturated 2 g	Sodium 110 mg
	saturated 0 g	Cholesterol 0 mg

Percentage of calories from fat: 23%
Diabetic exchanges: 1½ Starch/Bread; ½ Fat

Apple Raisin Scones

The perfect alternative to biscuits. Prepare these oat bran scones, sweetened naturally with apples and raisins. Serve with a hint of honey or preserves for extra flavor.

1½ cups all-purpose flour
¼ cup sugar
1 tablespoon baking powder
1 teaspoon cinnamon
⅓ cup (5⅓ tablespoons) margarine
1 cup Quaker Oat Bran hot cereal, uncooked

⅔ cup (3 oz.) finely chopped dried apples
½ cup raisins
⅓ cup water
2 egg whites, beaten

Heat oven to 400°F. Lightly spray cookie sheet with vegetable oil cooking spray or oil lightly. Combine flour, sugar, baking powder and cinnamon; cut in margarine until mixture resembles coarse crumbs. Stir in oat bran, apples and raisins. Add combined water and egg whites, mixing just until moistened. Shape dough to form a ball. Turn out onto lightly floured surface; knead gently 6 times. Pat into 9-inch circle on prepared cookie sheet. Score dough into eight wedges; do not separate. Bake 18 to 20 minutes or until light golden brown. Break apart; serve warm with jelly, jam or fruit preserves. *Makes 8 scones*

Nutrition information: Each serving (1 scone)

Calories 280	Fat 9 g	**Oat Bran 12 g**
Protein 6 g	polyunsaturated 2 g	Dietary Fiber 3 g
Carbohydrate 45 g	monounsaturated 5 g	Sodium 275 mg
	saturated 1 g	Cholesterol 0 mg

Percentage of calories from fat: 28%
Diabetic exchanges: 2 Starch/Bread; 1½ Fat; 1 Fruit

♥   ♥   ♥

Replace up to ⅓ the flour in your coffee cake or yeast bread recipes with oat bran. Depending on the amount of oat bran you wish to incorporate into your daily diet, substitute any percentage of oat bran for the flour up to, but not exceeding, one third.

Oat 'n Corn Bread

Enjoy the traditional goodness of plain corn bread. Or, add a spicy southwest twist to this hearty corn bread with chilies or bell peppers.

**1 cup Quaker Oat Bran hot
  cereal, uncooked
¾ cup Quaker or Aunt Jemima
  Enriched Corn Meal
¼ cup all-purpose flour
¼ cup sugar**

**4 teaspoons baking powder
¼ teaspoon salt (optional)
1 cup skim milk
3 tablespoons vegetable oil
1 egg white, slightly beaten**

Heat oven to 425°F. Lightly spray 8 or 9-inch square baking pan with vegetable oil cooking spray or oil lightly. Combine oat bran, corn meal, flour, sugar, baking powder and salt; add milk, oil and egg white, mixing well. Pour into prepared pan. Bake 20 to 25 minutes or until lightly browned. Serve warm.   *Makes 9 servings*

Variations: Add one 4-oz. can chopped green chilies, drained, or 1 cup finely chopped red bell pepper (about 1 medium) or combination of both with milk. Proceed as directed above.

Nutrition information: Each serving (⅑ of bread)

Calories 170	Fat 6 g	Oat Bran 9 g
Protein 5 g	polyunsaturated 3 g	Dietary Fiber 2 g
Carbohydrate 25 g	monounsaturated 1 g	Sodium 210 mg
	saturated 1 g	Cholesterol 0 mg

Percentage of calories from fat: 30%
Diabetic exchanges: 1½ Starch/Bread; 1 Fat

♥   ♥   ♥

**Replace up to ¼ the flour in your favorite biscuit
recipe with oat bran. Depending on the amount of oat
bran you wish to incorporate into your daily diet,
substitute any percentage of oat bran for the flour up
to, but not exceeding, one fourth.**

Entrees and accompaniments

Oat bran is no longer just for breakfast! The versatility of this remarkable grain makes it the perfect ingredient for a variety of entrees and side dishes. Try oat bran as a crisp coating for vegetables and meats, a topping for casseroles or as a hearty pizza crust.
Pictured here is Manicotti Florentine. See page 44 for recipe.

Manicotti Florentine

For oat bran with an Italian flair, try this delicious manicotti dish. A meatless entree with low fat cheeses and so easy in the microwave.

1 pkg. (10 oz.) frozen chopped spinach
½ cup chopped onion
1 clove garlic, minced
½ cup Quaker Oat Bran hot cereal, uncooked
½ cup low fat cottage cheese
1 teaspoon basil

½ teaspoon oregano
8 manicotti noodles, uncooked
2 cans (8 oz.) low sodium tomato sauce
1 teaspoon basil
¼ cup (1 oz.) shredded part skim mozzarella cheese

Heat oven to 375°F. Cook spinach according to package directions with onion and garlic. Cool slightly; drain. Stir in oat bran, cottage cheese, 1 teaspoon basil and oregano; set aside. Cook manicotti in boiling water 4 minutes; drain. Spread 1½ cans tomato sauce in bottom of 11×7-inch baking dish. Stuff each manicotti with about 3 tablespoons spinach mixture; arrange in baking dish. Pour remaining ½ can sauce over manicotti. Sprinkle with remaining 1 teaspoon basil. Top with mozzarella cheese. Cover; bake 25 to 30 minutes or until bubbly.

Makes 4 servings

MICROWAVE DIRECTIONS: Prepare as recipe directs; place in 11×7-inch microwaveable dish. *Do not* top manicotti with cheese. Cover with plastic wrap; vent. Microwave at HIGH 4 minutes. Remove plastic wrap; top with mozzarella cheese. Microwave at HIGH 2 to 3 minutes or until cheese is melted.

Nutrition information: Each serving (2 stuffed manicotti)

Calories 240	Fat 3 g	**Oat Bran 11 g**
Protein 14 g	polyunsaturated 1 g	Dietary Fiber 6 g
Carbohydrate 39 g	monounsaturated 0 g	Sodium 230 mg
	saturated 2 g	Cholesterol 5 mg

Percentage of calories from fat: 12%
Diabetic exchanges: 2 Starch/Bread; 2 Vegetable; ½ Medium Fat Meat

Crispy Lemon Sole

Enjoy your favorite fish fillet with this subtle lemon coating.

¾ cup Quaker Oat Bran hot
   cereal, uncooked
2 tablespoons grated parmesan
   cheese
1 tablespoon snipped fresh
   parsley or 1 teaspoon
   parsley flakes
½ teaspoon lemon pepper

½ teaspoon paprika
1 egg white, slightly beaten
¼ cup skim milk
1 lb. fresh or frozen sole or
   flounder fillets
3 tablespoons margarine,
   melted

Lightly spray rack of broiler pan with vegetable oil cooking spray or oil lightly. In shallow dish, combine oat bran, cheese, parsley, lemon pepper and paprika. In another shallow dish, combine egg white and milk. Coat fillets with oat bran mixture; shake off excess. Dip into egg mixture, then coat again with oat bran mixture. Place on prepared pan; drizzle with margarine. Broil about 4 inches from heat 4 to 5 minutes on each side or until golden brown. Garnish with lemon wedges, if desired.

Makes 5 servings

Note: See Herbed Baked Chicken (page 57) for convenient directions for snipping fresh parsley.

Nutrition information: Each serving (One 3-oz. portion)

Calories 210	Fat 10 g	**Oat Bran 12 g**
Protein 22 g	polyunsaturated 2 g	Dietary Fiber 2 g
Carbohydrate 8 g	monounsaturated 4 g	Sodium 300 mg
	saturated 2 g	Cholesterol 45 mg

Percentage of calories from fat: 42%
Diabetic exchanges: 3 Lean Meat; ½ Starch/Bread

Oat Bran
from the Expert ™

Sweet 'n Sour Pork

Gingered pork strips served over a bed of shredded cabbage makes an impressive dish.

¾ cup Quaker Oat Bran hot
    cereal, uncooked
1 teaspoon ginger
1 egg white
1 tablespoon water
¾ lb. pork tenderloin, cut into
    ⅛-inch-thick strips
3 tablespoons vegetable oil
1 can (10½ oz.) low sodium
    chicken broth

2 tablespoons cornstarch
1 can (8 oz.) pineapple tidbits in
    juice, undrained
1 medium green bell pepper,
    chopped
3 tablespoons firmly packed
    brown sugar
4 cups shredded cabbage
2 tablespoons white wine
    vinegar

In plastic bag, combine oat bran and ginger; mix well. In shallow dish, lightly beat egg white and water. Coat pork with oat bran mixture; shake off excess. Dip into egg mixture, then coat again with oat bran mixture. Saute pork in oil over medium-high heat 6 to 7 minutes or until meat is no longer pink. Remove from heat; keep warm.

Combine broth and cornstarch; mix until smooth. Add pineapple, pineapple juice, green pepper and brown sugar. Cook over medium heat about 4 minutes, stirring constantly or until sauce is clear and thickened. Remove from heat. Add cabbage and vinegar; mix well. To serve, spoon cabbage mixture onto serving platter; top with pork. Serve with rice or noodles, if desired.   *Makes 6 servings*

Nutrition information: Each serving (⅙ of recipe)

Calories 250	Fat 10 g	**Oat Bran 11 g**
Protein 16 g	polyunsaturated 5 g	Dietary Fiber 3 g
Carbohydrate 25 g	monounsaturated 2 g	Sodium 60 mg
	saturated 2 g	Cholesterol 35 mg

Percentage of calories from fat: 35%
Diabetic exchanges: 1½ Lean Meat; 1 Vegetable; 1 Starch/Bread; 1 Fat; ½ Fruit

Spicy Tomato Chicken

This sauce, prepared with tomato sauce and white wine, adds a spicy flavor to chicken breasts breaded with oat bran. Preparation time under 20 minutes.

½ cup Quaker Oat Bran hot cereal, uncooked
1½ teaspoons thyme leaves, crushed
1½ teaspoons garlic powder
⅛ to ¼ teaspoon ground red pepper
2 egg whites

2 chicken breasts, split, boned, skinned (about ¾ lb.)
2 tablespoons vegetable oil
¼ cup dry white wine
1 can (8 oz.) low sodium tomato sauce
½ cup sliced green onions

In shallow dish, combine oat bran, thyme, garlic powder and red pepper. In another shallow dish, lightly beat egg whites. Pound each chicken breast between sheets of waxed paper to even thickness. Coat with oat bran mixture; shake off excess. Dip into egg whites, then coat again with oat bran mixture. Saute chicken in oil over medium heat about 6 minutes; turn. Cook an additional 6 to 8 minutes or until juices run clear when pierced with fork. Remove to serving platter; keep warm.

Increase heat to high; add wine, mixing well with drippings. Add tomato sauce and green onions; heat through. Pour over chicken just before serving. Garnish with sliced green onions, if desired.

Makes 4 servings

Nutrition information: Each serving (1 breast)

Calories 230	Fat 9 g	**Oat Bran 11 g**
Protein 25 g	polyunsaturated 4 g	Dietary Fiber 3 g
Carbohydrate 12 g	monounsaturated 2 g	Sodium 95 mg
	saturated 2 g	Cholesterol 50 mg

Percentage of calories from fat: 35%
Diabetic exchanges: 3 Lean Meat; 1 Vegetable; ½ Starch/Bread

♥ ♥ ♥

Oat bran can be used to replace all of the flour, cracker crumbs, croutons, crushed cereal or bread crumbs in your favorite chicken, fish or vegetable coating, or savory vegetable topping.

Oat Bran 'n Broccoli Casserole

Team up healthful oat bran with a helping of grits, an old southern favorite, for a delicious side dish.

1 pkg. (10 oz.) frozen chopped
   broccoli
¾ cup water
⅓ cup sliced green onions
½ cup part skim ricotta cheese
¼ teaspoon garlic powder
   Dash of pepper
2 cups water

½ teaspoon salt (optional)
¾ cup Quaker Oat Bran hot
   cereal, uncooked
⅔ cup Quaker or Aunt Jemima
   Enriched Hominy Quick
   Grits*
½ cup plain low fat yogurt

Cook broccoli in ¾ cup water according to package directions with onions. Do not drain. Stir in ricotta, garlic powder and pepper. Cook over medium heat, stirring occasionally or until heated through; set aside.

Bring 2 cups water and salt to a boil. Using a wire whisk, gradually add combined oat bran and grits, stirring constantly. Return to a boil; reduce heat. Simmer 2 to 4 minutes, stirring frequently, or until oat bran mixture is slightly thickened. Add to broccoli mixture; mix well. Add yogurt; cook until heated through. Serve immediately.

Makes 6 servings

*To substitute Quaker or Aunt Jemima Enriched Hominy Grits, increase water to 2½ cups and simmer time to 15 to 20 minutes. Proceed as recipe directs.

Nutrition information: Each serving (about ¾ cup)

Calories 160	Fat 3 g	**Oat Bran 11 g**
Protein 8 g	polyunsaturated 1 g	Dietary Fiber 3 g
Carbohydrate 24 g	monounsaturated 1 g	Sodium 50 mg
	saturated 1 g	Cholesterol 5 mg

Percentage of calories from fat: 17%
Diabetic exchanges: 1 Starch/Bread; 1 Vegetable; ½ Lean Meat; ½ Fat

Zesty Italian Topper

The robust flavor of this topping gives an added punch to soups, pizza and side dishes. Use in place of traditional seasonings.

1 cup Quaker Oat Bran hot cereal, uncooked
3 tablespoons grated parmesan cheese

½ teaspoon Italian seasoning
¼ teaspoon garlic powder

Heat oven to 350°F. Place oat bran in ungreased 13×9-inch baking pan. Bake 15 to 17 minutes or until light golden brown, stirring occasionally. Cool; add parmesan cheese, Italian seasoning and garlic powder. Store tightly covered at room temperature. To serve, sprinkle generously on cooked vegetables, pizza, soups, salads or casseroles. Or, use as a coating for chicken, fish or vegetables. *Makes 1¼ cups*

MICROWAVE DIRECTIONS: Place oat bran in 1-qt. microwaveable bowl. Microwave at HIGH 2 to 3 minutes, stirring after every minute. Cool. Add parmesan cheese, Italian seasoning and garlic powder. Store tightly covered at room temperature. To serve, sprinkle generously on cooked vegetables, pizza, soups, salads or casseroles. Or, use as a coating for chicken, fish or vegetables.

Nutrition information: Each serving (1 tablespoon)

Calories 20	Fat 1 g	**Oat Bran 4 g**
Protein 1 g	polyunsaturated 0 g	Dietary Fiber 1 g
Carbohydrate 2 g	monounsaturated 0 g	Sodium 15 mg
	saturated 0 g	Cholesterol 0 mg

Percentage of calories from fat: 26%
Diabetic exchanges: ¼ Starch/Bread

♥   ♥   ♥

Sprinkle uncooked Quaker Oat Bran hot cereal and 1 to 2 teaspoons melted margarine over casseroles in place of potato chips, croutons or bread crumbs.

Vegetable Pizza with Oat Bran Crust

At last, pizza you can indulge in to your heart's content! Try your favorite combination of fresh vegetables to top this golden brown crust made with oat bran.

1 cup Quaker Oat Bran hot cereal, uncooked
1 cup all-purpose flour
1 teaspoon baking powder
¾ cup skim milk
3 tablespoons vegetable oil
1 tablespoon Quaker Oat Bran hot cereal, uncooked
1 can (8 oz.) low sodium tomato sauce

1 cup sliced mushrooms (about 3 oz.)
1 medium green, red or yellow bell pepper or combination, cut into rings
½ cup chopped onion
1¼ cups (5 oz.) shredded part skim mozzarella cheese
½ teaspoon oregano leaves or Italian seasoning, crushed

Combine 1 cup oat bran, flour and baking powder. Add milk and oil; mix well. Let stand 10 minutes.

Heat oven to 425°F. Lightly spray 12-inch round pizza pan with vegetable oil cooking spray or oil lightly. Sprinkle with 1 tablespoon oat bran. With lightly oiled fingers, pat dough out evenly; shape edge to form rim. Bake 18 to 20 minutes. Spread sauce evenly over partially baked crust. Top with vegetables; sprinkle with cheese and oregano. Bake an additional 12 to 15 minutes or until golden brown. Cut into 8 wedges.

Makes 4 servings

Nutrition information: Each serving (¼ of pizza)

Calories 440	Fat 19 g	**Oat Bran 21 g**
Protein 19 g	polyunsaturated 7 g	Dietary Fiber 6 g
Carbohydrate 48 g	monounsaturated 5 g	Sodium 300 mg
	saturated 6 g	Cholesterol 20 mg

Percentage of calories from fat: 38%
Diabetic exchanges: 3 Vegetable; 3 Fat; 2 Starch/Bread; 1 Lean Meat

Vegetable Pizza with Oat Bran Crust

Golden Oats Pilaf

This colorful combination of oat bran, oats and a variety of fresh vegetables makes a wonderful side dish.

1½ cups Old Fashioned Quaker Oats, uncooked*
⅓ cup Quaker Oat Bran hot cereal, uncooked
3 egg whites
½ teaspoon salt (optional)
1 cup quartered mushrooms (about 3 oz.)

1 small green bell pepper, chopped
½ cup sliced green onions
1 tablespoon liquid vegetable oil margarine
1 can (10½ oz.) low sodium chicken broth
1 medium tomato, chopped

Combine oats, oat bran, egg whites and salt until oats are evenly coated; set aside. Saute mushrooms, green pepper and onions in margarine over medium-high heat 2 to 3 minutes or until vegetables are crisp-tender. Add oat mixture; cook over medium heat about 5 to 6 minutes, stirring constantly, or until oats are dry, separated and lightly browned.

Add broth; continue cooking 2 to 3 minutes or until liquid is absorbed. Stir in tomato; serve immediately. *Makes 6 servings*

*To substitute 1½ cups Quick Quaker Oats, uncooked, reduce chicken broth to 1 cup. Proceed as directed above.

Nutrition information: Each serving (¾ cup)

Calories 140	Fat 4 g	**Oat Bran 11 g**
Protein 7 g	polyunsaturated 2 g	Dietary Fiber 3 g
Carbohydrate 19 g	monounsaturated 1 g	Sodium 55 mg
	saturated 1 g	Cholesterol 0 mg

Percentage of calories from fat: 26%
Diabetic exchanges: 2 Vegetable; 1 Starch/Bread; 1 Fat

Zucchini Bake

This versatile casserole may be used as a light entree.

⅔ cup Quaker Oat Bran hot
    cereal, uncooked
½ teaspoon Italian seasoning
¼ teaspoon pepper
1 egg white
1 tablespoon water
2 medium zucchini, sliced
    ¾ inch thick, quartered
    (about 3 cups)

1 small onion, chopped
⅔ cup low sodium tomato sauce
2 teaspoons olive oil
2 teaspoons grated parmesan
    cheese
¼ cup (1 oz.) shredded part skim
    mozzarella cheese

Heat oven to 375°F. Lightly spray 8-inch square baking dish with vegetable oil cooking spray or oil lightly. In plastic bag, combine oat bran, Italian seasoning and pepper; mix well. In shallow dish, lightly beat egg white and water. Coat zucchini with oat bran mixture; shake off excess. Dip into egg mixture, then coat again with oat bran mixture. Place zucchini in prepared dish; sprinkle with onion. Spoon combined tomato sauce and oil over vegetables. Sprinkle with parmesan cheese. Bake about 30 minutes or until zucchini is crisp-tender; top with mozzarella cheese. Serve warm. *Makes 9 side-dish or 3 main-dish servings*

MICROWAVE DIRECTIONS: In plastic bag, combine oat bran, Italian seasoning and pepper; mix well. In shallow dish, lightly beat egg white and water. Coat zucchini with oat bran mixture; shake off excess. Dip into egg mixture, then coat again with oat bran mixture. Place zucchini in 8-inch square microwaveable dish; sprinkle with onion. Spoon combined tomato sauce and oil over vegetables. Sprinkle with parmesan cheese. Microwave at HIGH 5 minutes 30 seconds to 6 minutes 30 seconds or until zucchini is crisp-tender, rotating dish ½ turn after 3 minutes. Sprinkle with mozzarella cheese. Let stand 3 minutes before serving. Serve warm.

Nutrition information: Each side-dish serving (1/9 of recipe)

Calories 60	Fat 2 g	**Oat Bran 6 g**
Protein 3 g	polyunsaturated 0 g	Dietary Fiber 1 g
Carbohydrate 7 g	monounsaturated 1 g	Sodium 35 mg
	saturated 0 g	Cholesterol 0 mg

Percentage of calories from fat: 34%
Diabetic exchanges: ½ Starch/Bread; ½ Fat

Herbed Baked Chicken

A quick and easy recipe for a lightly seasoned, moist chicken breast with fresh parsley. A great alternative to traditional fried chicken.

¾ cup Quaker Oat Bran hot cereal, uncooked
¼ teaspoon garlic powder
¼ teaspoon pepper
¼ teaspoon salt (optional)
1 egg white, slightly beaten
1 tablespoon water

3 chicken breasts, split, boned, skinned (about 1 lb.)
2 tablespoons liquid vegetable oil margarine
¼ cup snipped fresh parsley or 1½ teaspoons parsley flakes

Heat oven to 350°F. In shallow dish, combine oat bran, garlic powder, pepper and salt; mix well. In another shallow dish, lightly beat egg white and water. Dip chicken into egg mixture, then coat with oat bran mixture. Place on wire rack in 15×10-inch foil-lined baking pan. Drizzle with margarine. Bake 45 to 50 minutes or until chicken is tender and coating is lightly browned. Remove chicken to serving platter. Top with parsley. Squeeze lemon wedge over chicken before serving, if desired.

Makes 6 servings

Tip
To snip fresh parsley: Rinse with cool water and dry thoroughly. Remove stems; place parsley tops in short plastic cup. Using kitchen shears, snip parsley until well chopped.

Nutrition information: Each serving (1 breast)

Calories 160	Fat 5 g	**Oat Bran 16 g**
Protein 20 g	polyunsaturated 2 g	Dietary Fiber 2 g
Carbohydrate 6 g	monounsaturated 1 g	Sodium 85 mg
	saturated 2 g	Cholesterol 45 mg

Percentage of calories from fat: 32%
Diabetic exchanges: 2½ Lean Meat; ½ Starch/Bread

Eggplant Italiano

Eggplant Italiano, with the added benefit of oat bran and low fat cheese, never tasted so good. Serve as a light lunch or dinner side dish.

1 eggplant (1 lb.), peeled if desired
1 can (6 oz.) low sodium cocktail vegetable juice (¾ cup)
½ cup Quaker Oat Bran hot cereal, uncooked
2 garlic cloves, minced

1 teaspoon basil leaves, crushed
½ teaspoon oregano
2 medium tomatoes, chopped
1¼ cups (5 oz.) shredded part skim mozzarella cheese

Heat oven to 350°F. Line cookie sheet or 15×10-inch baking pan with foil. Lightly spray with vegetable oil cooking spray or oil lightly. Cut eggplant into ½-inch-thick slices; place in single layer on prepared pan. Combine vegetable juice, oat bran, garlic, basil and oregano. Spread evenly over eggplant; top with tomatoes. Sprinkle with mozzarella cheese. Bake 35 to 40 minutes or until eggplant is tender and cheese is melted. Sprinkle with additional basil or oregano, if desired.

Makes 4 main-dish or 8 side-dish servings

Tip
Eggplant is in season throughout the year. Select an eggplant with a smooth, firm and evenly colored skin, a bright green cap and one that is free of scars.

Nutrition information: Each main-dish serving (¼ of recipe)

Calories 190	Fat 7 g	**Oat Bran 11 g**
Protein 13 g	polyunsaturated 0 g	Dietary Fiber 4 g
Carbohydrate 20 g	monounsaturated 2 g	Sodium 190 mg
	saturated 4 g	Cholesterol 20 mg

Percentage of calories from fat: 32%
Diabetic exchanges: 1 Starch/Bread; 1 Lean Meat; 1 Vegetable; ½ Fat

♥　♥　♥

Combine 2 tablespoons uncooked Quaker Oat Bran hot cereal and 1/2 teaspoon snipped fresh parsley; sprinkle over broiled or baked tomatoes topped with low fat cheddar or ricotta cheese.

Savory Oat Bran Topping

The spicy flavor of this topping can be sprinkled over vegetables or used as a coating for skinless chicken. This is an easy way to add oat bran to your diet.

1 cup Quaker Oat Bran hot
  cereal, uncooked
1 tablespoon snipped fresh
  parsley or 1 teaspoon
  parsley flakes

1 teaspoon grated lemon peel
  (optional)
3 tablespoons grated parmesan
  cheese
½ teaspoon pepper

Heat oven to 350°F. Place oat bran in ungreased 13×9-inch baking pan. Bake 15 to 17 minutes or until light golden brown, stirring occasionally. Stir in parsley and lemon peel; cool. Add parmesan cheese and pepper. Store tightly covered at room temperature. To serve, sprinkle generously on cooked vegetables, pizza, soups, salads or casseroles. Or, use as a coating for chicken, fish or vegetables.   *Makes 1¼ cups*

MICROWAVE DIRECTIONS: Place oat bran in 1-qt. microwaveable bowl. Microwave at HIGH 2 to 3 minutes, stirring after every minute. Add parsley and lemon peel; cool. Add parmesan cheese and pepper. Store tightly covered at room temperature. To serve, sprinkle generously on cooked vegetables, pizza, soups, salads or casseroles. Or, use as a coating for chicken, fish or vegetables.

Note: See Herbed Baked Chicken (page 57) for convenient directions for snipping fresh parsley.

Nutrition information: Each serving (1 tablespoon)

Calories 20	Fat 1 g	**Oat Bran 4 g**
Protein 1 g	polyunsaturated 0 g	Dietary Fiber 1 g
Carbohydrate 2 g	monounsaturated 0 g	Sodium 15 mg
	saturated 0 g	Cholesterol 0 mg

Percentage of calories from fat: 26%
Diabetic exchanges: ¼ Starch/Bread

Turkey Cutlets

Just coat and bake for delicious, moist turkey cutlets. Drizzle with cranberry orange relish for a tangy sweet twist.

¾ cup Quaker Oat Bran hot cereal, uncooked
1 tablespoon snipped fresh parsley or 1 teaspoon parsley flakes
1½ teaspoons grated orange peel (optional)
¼ teaspoon sage

⅓ cup orange juice
1 egg white, slightly beaten
1 lb. fresh turkey cutlets
2 tablespoons margarine, melted
½ cup whole berry cranberry sauce

Heat oven to 375°F. Lightly spray rack of foil-lined broiler pan with vegetable oil cooking spray or oil lightly. In shallow dish, combine oat bran, parsley, orange peel and sage; mix well. In another shallow dish, combine orange juice and egg white; mix well. Dip each cutlet into orange juice mixture, then coat with oat bran mixture. Place on prepared rack. Bake 20 minutes; turn. Drizzle with margarine; bake an additional 15 minutes or until juices run clear when pierced with fork. Serve each cutlet with 2 tablespoons cranberry sauce.   *Makes 4 servings*

Note: See Herbed Baked Chicken (page 57) for convenient directions for snipping fresh parsley.

Nutrition information: Each serving (2 cutlets)

Calories 310	Fat 9 g	**Oat Bran 19 g**
Protein 31 g	polyunsaturated 2 g	Dietary Fiber 2 g
Carbohydrate 25 g	monounsaturated 3 g	Sodium 170 mg
	saturated 2 g	Cholesterol 70 mg

Percentage of calories from fat: 26%
Diabetic exchanges: 3½ Lean Meat; 1 Fruit; 1 Starch/Bread

**Oat Bran
from the Expert** ™

Indian Chicken Crepes

Curry, peanuts and raisins are popular flavors of Indian cooking and make a sensational filling for these healthful oat bran crepes.

1½ cups chopped cooked chicken
1 carton (8 oz.) plain low fat yogurt
2 tablespoons raisins
2 tablespoons sliced green onion
2 tablespoons chopped sweet pickle
½ to 1 teaspoon curry powder (optional)

⅛ teaspoon ground red pepper
¾ cup Quaker Oat Bran hot cereal, uncooked
1 teaspoon baking powder
1 cup skim milk
3 egg whites, slightly beaten
1 tablespoon liquid vegetable oil margarine
⅓ cup chopped dry roasted peanuts

Combine chicken, yogurt, raisins, onion, pickle, curry powder and red pepper; mix well. Cover; chill.

Combine oat bran and baking powder; add combined milk, egg whites and margarine, mixing well. Heat 6 to 7-inch crepe pan or skillet over medium heat. Lightly spray with vegetable oil cooking spray or oil lightly before making each crepe. Pour about ¼ cup batter onto hot prepared pan; immediately tilt pan to coat bottom evenly. Cook 1 to 1½ minutes or until top looks dry. Turn; cook an additional 1 minute. Cool. Stack between sheets of waxed paper.

Stir peanuts into chicken mixture just before serving. Spoon about 2 tablespoons filling along less evenly browned side of each crepe. Fold or roll up sides to cover filling. Serve immediately.   *Makes 5 servings*

Note: See Apple Raisin Crepes (page 22) for freezing and reheating tips on crepes.

Tip
To cook chicken in microwave oven: Arrange split, boned and skinned chicken breasts in 9 or 10-inch microwaveable pie plate with meatiest portions toward outside edge of dish. Tuck under thin portions for more even thickness. Cover with plastic wrap; vent. Microwave at HIGH 4 to 5 minutes per pound or until juices run clear when pierced with fork, turning dish and rearranging chicken after 2 minutes.

Nutrition information: Each serving (2 crepes)

Calories 280	Fat 13 g	**Oat Bran 13 g**
Protein 23 g	polyunsaturated 4 g	Dietary Fiber 3 g
Carbohydrate 20 g	monounsaturated 5 g	Sodium 275 mg
	saturated 3 g	Cholesterol 40 mg

Percentage of calories from fat: 40%
Diabetic exchanges: 3 Lean Meat; 1 Fat

Indian Chicken Crepes

BBQ Meat Loaf

The barbecue sauce adds tangy flavor to this all-time favorite dish made healthy with oat bran and extra lean ground beef. Try microwave preparation for an easy weekday dinner.

⅔ cup skim milk
3 egg whites, slightly beaten
½ cup finely chopped celery
½ cup chopped onion
¼ cup snipped fresh parsley or
    1½ teaspoons parsley
    flakes
½ teaspoon sage
¼ teaspoon salt (optional)

¼ teaspoon pepper
1 lb. extra lean ground beef
1 cup Quaker Oat Bran hot
    cereal, uncooked
¼ cup catsup
2 tablespoons firmly packed
    brown sugar
1 teaspoon dry mustard

Heat oven to 350°F. Combine milk, egg whites, vegetables and seasonings; mix well. Add ground beef and oat bran; mix lightly but thoroughly. Press into 8×4-inch loaf pan. Bake 50 minutes. Combine catsup, brown sugar and mustard; mix well. Spoon over meat; bake an additional 10 minutes. Let stand 5 minutes before serving.

Makes 6 servings

MICROWAVE DIRECTIONS: Combine milk, egg whites, vegetables and seasonings; mix well. Add ground beef and oat bran; mix lightly but thoroughly. Press into 5½-cup ring mold. Invert onto 9 or 10-inch glass pie plate; remove mold. Cover with waxed paper. Microwave at HIGH 11 to 12 minutes or until edges are lightly browned and center is no longer pink, turning dish ¼ turn every 3 minutes. Combine catsup, brown sugar and mustard; mix well. Spoon over meat. Let stand 5 minutes.

Variation: For Microwave Mini-Loaf, prepare as directed above. Divide ground beef mixture into 3 equal parts; shape into loaves. Place into 11×7-inch microwaveable dish. Cover with waxed paper. Microwave at HIGH 11 minutes to 11 minutes 30 seconds or until edges are lightly browned and center is no longer pink, turning dish after 5 minutes. Combine catsup, brown sugar and mustard; mix well. Spoon over meat. Let stand 5 minutes.

Note: See Herbed Baked Chicken (page 57) for convenient directions for snipping fresh parsley.

Nutrition information: Each serving (⅙ of loaf)

Calories 290	Fat 14 g	Oat Bran 14 g
Protein 20 g	polyunsaturated 2 g	Dietary Fiber 3 g
Carbohydrate 18 g	monounsaturated 6 g	Sodium 220 mg
	saturated 5 g	Cholesterol 50 mg

Percentage of calories from fat: 45%
Diabetic exchanges: 3 Fat; 2 Lean Meat; 2 Vegetable; ½ Starch/Bread

BBQ Meat Loaf with
Crispened New Potatoes (see page 66)

Crispened New Potatoes

This versatile side dish is a new way to prepare an old favorite. Try these new potatoes with a crispy coating of oat bran.

1½ lbs. very small, scrubbed new potatoes (about 12)	**½ teaspoon snipped fresh dill or ½ teaspoon dill weed**
½ cup Quaker Oat Bran hot cereal, uncooked	**½ teaspoon paprika**
2 tablespoons grated parmesan cheese	**1 egg white, slightly beaten**
1 tablespoon snipped fresh parsley or 1 teaspoon parsley flakes	**¼ cup skim milk**
	1 tablespoon margarine, melted

Heat oven to 400°F. Lightly spray 11×7-inch baking dish with vegetable oil cooking spray or oil lightly. Cook whole potatoes in boiling water 15 minutes. Drain; rinse in cold water.

In shallow dish, combine oat bran, cheese, parsley, dill and paprika. In another shallow dish, combine egg white and milk. Coat each potato in oat bran mixture; shake off excess. Dip into egg mixture, then coat again with oat bran mixture. Place into prepared dish; drizzle with margarine. Cover; bake 10 minutes. Uncover; bake an additional 10 minutes or until potatoes are tender.   *Makes 4 servings*

Note: See Herbed Baked Chicken (page 57) for convenient directions for snipping fresh parsley.

Nutrition information: Each serving (3 potatoes)

Calories 230	Fat 5 g	**Oat Bran 11 g**
Protein 8 g	polyunsaturated 1 g	Dietary Fiber 4 g
Carbohydrate 38 g	monounsaturated 2 g	Sodium 110 mg
	saturated 1 g	Cholesterol 0 mg

Percentage of calories from fat: 19%
Diabetic exchanges: 2 Starch/Bread; 1 Fat

Dilled Tuna Patties with Veggie Yogurt Sauce

The tart vegetable sauce, made with a yogurt base, is the perfect complement to these golden brown patties. Try salmon in place of tuna for a tasty variation.

1 carton (8 oz.) plain low fat yogurt
⅓ cup grated carrot
2 tablespoons chopped celery
1 tablespoon chopped green onion
¼ teaspoon dill weed
2 cans (6½ oz.) chunk light tuna in water, drained, flaked

½ cup Quaker Oat Bran hot cereal, uncooked
1 egg white, slightly beaten
2 tablespoons chopped green onion
¼ teaspoon dill weed
2 tablespoons vegetable oil

Combine ½ cup yogurt, carrot, celery, 1 tablespoon green onion and ¼ teaspoon dill; mix well. Cover; chill.

Combine tuna, oat bran, remaining yogurt, egg white, 2 tablespoons green onion and ¼ teaspoon dill; mix well. Shape to form 6 patties. Saute in oil over medium heat 3 to 4 minutes on each side or until golden brown. Serve each patty with 2 tablespoons yogurt sauce.

Makes 6 servings

Variation: Substitute two 7½-oz. cans or one 15-oz. can salmon, drained, boned and skinned for tuna.

Nutrition information: Each serving (1 patty)

Calories 170	Fat 6 g	**Oat Bran 8 g**
Protein 20 g	polyunsaturated 3 g	Dietary Fiber 1 g
Carbohydrate 8 g	monounsaturated 1 g	Sodium 230 mg
	saturated 1 g	Cholesterol 25 mg

Percentage of calories from fat: 33%
Diabetic exchanges: 2½ Lean Meat; ½ Vegetable; ½ Starch/Bread

---

♥   ♥   ♥

**Add 1 cup uncooked Quaker Oat Bran hot cereal and
2/3 cup skim milk or water to 1 pound extra lean
ground beef for meat loaf, hamburgers or meatballs.**

Sweet temptations

Dessert has been both the most tempting and forbidden part of any meal. There is no longer any reason to pass by these treats! Prepared with oat bran, the following desserts are low in fat, calories and cholesterol— and taste sensational. Choose from elegant Berry and Apricot Crepes, easy-to-prepare Very Strawberry Shortcakes or traditional and homey Pineapple Upside Down Cake. Enjoy! Pictured here are Berry and Apricot Crepes. See page 70 for recipe.

Berry and Apricot Crepes

Fresh fruit and a hint of mint provide just the right touch to this elegant dessert. Freeze the remaining crepes for a dessert later in the week.

¾ cup Quaker Oat Bran hot
   cereal, uncooked
1 teaspoon baking powder
1 cup skim milk
3 egg whites, slightly beaten
1 tablespoon liquid vegetable oil
   margarine
1 jar (12 oz.) apricot preserves
2 tablespoons dry white wine or
   apple juice

2 cups sliced strawberries
   (about 1 pint)
¾ cup fresh or thawed frozen
   blueberries
1 tablespoon chopped fresh
   mint or 1 teaspoon mint
   leaves

Combine oat bran and baking powder; add combined milk, egg whites and margarine, mixing well. Heat 6 to 7-inch crepe pan or skillet over medium heat. Lightly spray with vegetable oil cooking spray or oil lightly before making each crepe. Pour about ¼ cup batter onto hot prepared pan; immediately tilt pan to coat bottom evenly. Cook 1 to 1½ minutes or until top looks dry. Turn; cook an additional 1 minute. Cool. Layer between sheets of waxed paper.

Combine preserves and wine; mix well. Combine 3 tablespoons preserve mixture, strawberries, blueberries and mint; mix lightly. Spoon about 2 tablespoons fruit mixture along less evenly browned side of each crepe. Fold or roll up sides to cover filling. Top each serving with 2 tablespoons remaining preserve mixture. Garnish with whole strawberries, blueberries and fresh mint, if desired. Serve immediately.

Makes 5 servings

Note: See Apple Raisin Crepes (page 22) for freezing and reheating tips on crepes.

Nutrition information: Each serving (2 crepes)

Calories 320	Fat 4 g	**Oat Bran 13 g**
Protein 7 g	polyunsaturated 2 g	Dietary Fiber 4 g
Carbohydrate 65 g	monounsaturated 1 g	Sodium 170 mg
	saturated 1 g	Cholesterol 0 mg

Percentage of calories from fat: 12%
Diabetic exchanges: 3 Fruit; 1 Starch/Bread; 1 Fat

Pineapple Upside Down Cake

This light and moist cake, with an oat topping, is a tasteful alternative to the traditional pineapple upside down cake.

1 can (8 oz.) pineapple slices in juice, undrained
2 tablespoons liquid vegetable oil margarine
¼ cup firmly packed brown sugar
2 maraschino cherries, cut in half (optional)
¾ cup Quaker Oats (quick or old fashioned, uncooked)

1 cup granulated sugar
¼ cup liquid vegetable oil margarine
2 egg whites, slightly beaten
1 teaspoon vanilla
1 cup all-purpose flour
½ cup Quaker Oat Bran hot cereal, uncooked
2 teaspoons baking powder

Heat oven to 350°F. Drain pineapple, reserving juice. In 8 or 9-inch square baking pan, heat 2 tablespoons margarine. Add 1 tablespoon pineapple juice and brown sugar; mix well. Arrange pineapple in pan. Place cherry half in center of each pineapple. Sprinkle oats evenly over juice mixture and pineapple.

Beat granulated sugar and ¼ cup margarine until well blended. Add water to remaining pineapple juice to measure ½ cup. Add combined pineapple juice, egg whites and vanilla; mix well. Add combined flour, oat bran and baking powder, mixing until well blended. Carefully pour batter over oats; spread to edge of pan. Bake 40 to 45 minutes or until wooden pick inserted in center comes out clean. Cool on wire rack 5 minutes; invert onto serving platter. Cool completely before serving.

Makes 9 servings

Nutrition information: Each serving (1/9 of recipe)

Calories 290	Fat 8 g	**Oat Bran 5 g**
Protein 4 g	polyunsaturated 4 g	Dietary Fiber 2 g
Carbohydrate 50 g	monounsaturated 2 g	Sodium 180 mg
	saturated 1 g	Cholesterol 0 mg

Percentage of calories from fat: 26%
Diabetic exchanges: 2 Fruit; 1½ Starch/Bread; 1½ Fat

❤   ❤   ❤

Sprinkle desired amount of uncooked Quaker Oat Bran hot cereal over unbaked coffee cake, muffin or cupcake batter. Bake as recipe directs.

Very Strawberry Shortcakes

A truly sensational treat! Made with oat bran and sweetened with fresh fruit, there is no longer any reason to skip dessert.

2½ cups sliced strawberries
    (about 1 pint)
1 tablespoon sugar
1 tablespoon orange-flavored
    liqueur (optional)
1½ cups all-purpose flour
  ½ cup Quaker Oat Bran hot
    cereal, uncooked

3 tablespoons sugar
2 teaspoons baking powder
½ teaspoon salt (optional)
⅔ cup skim milk
3 tablespoons vegetable oil
2 cups dessert topping mix
    prepared with skim milk

Combine strawberries, 1 tablespoon sugar and liqueur; mix well. Cover; chill at least 1 hour.

Heat oven to 375°F. Lightly spray cookie sheet with vegetable oil cooking spray or oil lightly. Combine flour, oat bran, 3 tablespoons sugar, baking powder and salt; mix well. Add combined milk and oil, stirring with fork until mixture leaves sides of bowl and forms a ball. Drop six 3-inch dough balls onto prepared cookie sheet. Bake 20 to 22 minutes or until light golden brown. Cool 1 minute on cookie sheet; remove to wire rack. Cool completely.

Split each shortcake in half crosswise. Spoon ¼ cup strawberry mixture onto bottom halves of six shortcakes. Top each with ¼ cup dessert topping and remaining shortcake halves. Garnish with remaining strawberries and dessert topping.   *Makes 6 servings*

Nutrition information: Each serving (1 shortcake)

Calories 310	Fat 10 g	**Oat Bran 7 g**
Protein 7 g	polyunsaturated 4 g	Dietary Fiber 4 g
Carbohydrate 47 g	monounsaturated 2 g	Sodium 180 mg
	saturated 3 g	Cholesterol 0 mg

Percentage of calories from fat: 30%
Diabetic exchanges: 2 Fruit; 2 Fat; 1 Starch/Bread

Very Strawberry Shortcake

Carrot Pudding Cake with Lemon Sauce

Finally, a luscious dessert that's healthy! Moist and rich, serve this impressive cake to family and friends.

¼ cup liquid vegetable oil margarine
⅓ cup firmly packed brown sugar
½ cup frozen apple juice concentrate, thawed
3 egg whites, slightly beaten
1 cup Quaker Oat Bran hot cereal, uncooked
½ cup all-purpose flour
2 teaspoons baking powder
1 teaspoon cinnamon

2 cups finely shredded carrots (about 4 or 5 medium)
½ cup granulated sugar
4 teaspoons cornstarch
1 cup hot water
1 tablespoon liquid vegetable oil margarine
1 tablespoon lemon juice
½ teaspoon grated lemon peel
1 drop yellow food coloring (optional)

Heat oven to 325°F. Lightly spray 1½ or 2-qt. casserole with vegetable oil cooking spray or oil lightly. Combine ¼ cup margarine and brown sugar. Add apple juice concentrate and egg whites, mixing well. Add combined oat bran, flour, baking powder and cinnamon; mix well. Stir in carrots; pour into prepared dish. Bake 45 to 50 minutes or until edges are lightly browned and center is firm. Cool on wire rack about 1 hour.

Combine granulated sugar and cornstarch. Gradually add water, mixing until sugar dissolves. Cook over medium heat about 3 minutes, stirring constantly or until thickened and clear. Remove from heat; stir in 1 tablespoon margarine, lemon juice, lemon peel and food coloring; cool slightly. Spoon 2 tablespoons lemon sauce over each serving.

Makes 8 servings

MICROWAVE LEMON SAUCE DIRECTIONS: In 4-cup microwaveable measuring cup, combine granulated sugar and cornstarch. Gradually add water, mixing until sugar dissolves. Microwave at HIGH 2 to 3 minutes or until sauce is clear and thickened, stirring after every minute. Add margarine, lemon juice, lemon peel and food coloring, mixing well. Cool slightly.

Nutrition information: Each serving (⅛ of recipe)

Calories 270	Fat 8 g	Oat Bran 11 g
Protein 5 g	polyunsaturated 5 g	Dietary Fiber 3 g
Carbohydrate 45 g	monounsaturated 2 g	Sodium 200 mg
	saturated 1 g	Cholesterol 0 mg

Percentage of calories from fat: 26%
Diabetic exchanges: 2 Fruit; 1½ Fat; 1 Starch/Bread

Carrot Pudding Cake with Lemon Sauce

Pear 'n Raisin Crisp

Serve this tempting dessert warm with vanilla yogurt or ice milk. Vary your choice of fruit with the changing seasons.

½ cup Quaker Oat Bran hot
   cereal, uncooked
2 tablespoons firmly packed
   brown sugar
½ teaspoon cinnamon
1 tablespoon margarine, melted
6 cups peeled, sliced pears
   (about 6 medium)*

½ cup raisins
¼ cup water
1 tablespoon lemon juice
¼ cup firmly packed brown
   sugar
2 tablespoons all-purpose flour
½ teaspoon cinnamon

Heat oven to 375°F. Combine oat bran, 2 tablespoons brown sugar, ½ teaspoon cinnamon and margarine; mix well. Set aside.

Combine pears, raisins, water and lemon juice. Add combined ¼ cup brown sugar, flour and ½ teaspoon cinnamon, stirring until pears are evenly coated. Arrange in 8-inch square baking dish; sprinkle oat bran mixture evenly over pears. Bake 25 to 30 minutes or until fruit is tender.

*Substitute 6 cups peeled, sliced apples or peaches for pears.

Makes 8 servings

MICROWAVE DIRECTIONS: In 1-qt. microwaveable bowl, combine oat bran, 2 tablespoons brown sugar, ½ teaspoon cinnamon and margarine; mix well. Microwave at HIGH 2 to 3 minutes or until mixture resembles coarse crumbs, stirring after every minute. Cool completely.

Combine pears, raisins, water and lemon juice. Add combined ¼ cup brown sugar, flour and ½ teaspoon cinnamon, stirring until pears are evenly coated. Arrange in 8-inch square microwaveable dish. Cover with plastic wrap; vent. Microwave at HIGH 7 to 9 minutes, stirring after 4 minutes. Sprinkle oat bran mixture evenly over pears. Microwave at HIGH 1 to 2 minutes or until fruit is tender.

Nutrition information: Each serving (¾ cup)

Calories 180	Fat 2 g	**Oat Bran 4 g**
Protein 2 g	polyunsaturated 1 g	Dietary Fiber 4 g
Carbohydrate 41 g	monounsaturated 1 g	Sodium 20 mg
	saturated 0 g	Cholesterol 0 mg

Percentage of calories from fat: 11%
Diabetic exchanges: 2 Fruit; 1 Starch/Bread; ½ Fat

Blueberry Bran Bars

Serve this healthy treat as a snack or dessert. Pack a couple in your lunch bag for a delicious afternoon treat.

1¾ cups Quaker Oats (quick or old fashioned, uncooked)
1 cup Quaker Oat Bran hot cereal, uncooked
½ cup all-purpose flour
½ cup firmly packed brown sugar
½ teaspoon baking powder
¼ teaspoon salt (optional)

⅓ cup liquid vegetable oil margarine
⅓ cup light corn syrup
2 cups fresh or frozen blueberries (about 1 pint)
½ cup granulated sugar
3 tablespoons water
2 tablespoons cornstarch
2 teaspoons lemon juice

Heat oven to 350°F. Lightly spray 11×7-inch baking dish with vegetable oil cooking spray or oil lightly. Combine oats, oat bran, flour, brown sugar, baking powder and salt. Add margarine and corn syrup, mixing until mixture resembles coarse crumbs; reserve 1 cup. Press remaining mixture onto bottom of prepared dish. Bake 10 minutes.

Combine blueberries, granulated sugar and 2 tablespoons water. Bring to a boil; simmer 2 minutes, uncovered, stirring occasionally. Combine remaining 1 tablespoon water, cornstarch and lemon juice; mix well. Gradually stir into blueberry mixture; cook and stir about 30 seconds or until thickened and clear. Spread over partially baked base to within ¼ inch of edge; sprinkle with reserved oat mixture. Bake 18 to 20 minutes or until topping is lightly browned. Cool on wire rack; cut into bars. Store loosely covered. *Makes 15 bars*

Nutrition information: Each serving (¹⁄₁₅ of recipe)

Calories 200	Fat 5 g	**Oat Bran 6 g**
Protein 3 g	polyunsaturated 2 g	Dietary Fiber 2 g
Carbohydrate 36 g	monounsaturated 1 g	Sodium 55 mg
	saturated 1 g	Cholesterol 0 mg

Percentage of calories from fat: 23%
Diabetic exchanges: 1½ Fruit; 1 Starch/Bread; 1 Fat

Cocoa Waffles

These versatile cocoa treats are a favorite with kids. Top with powdered sugar, fruit or try making a healthy ice cream sandwich.

2 egg whites
1 cup all-purpose flour
¾ cup Quaker Oat Bran hot cereal, uncooked
½ cup sugar
¼ cup cocoa
1 teaspoon cinnamon
½ teaspoon baking soda
½ teaspoon baking powder
¼ teaspoon salt (optional)
1¼ cups skim milk
3 tablespoons vegetable oil

Heat waffle iron according to manufacturer's instructions. Beat egg whites until soft peaks form; set aside. Combine flour, oat bran, sugar, cocoa, cinnamon, baking soda, baking powder and salt; mix well. Whisk milk and oil until well blended. Add to dry ingredients, mixing just until moistened. Do not overmix. Fold egg whites into batter. Pour about 1 cup batter onto surface of grid. Close the lid; bake until steam no longer escapes from the sides of the iron and waffles are deep brown. Serve with fruit, powdered sugar, ice milk or low fat frozen yogurt, if desired.

Makes 6 servings

Variation: For Frozen Waffle Sandwiches, cut waffles in half lengthwise. Cut ice milk or frozen yogurt into ½-inch-thick rectangular slices, slightly smaller in size than waffle halves. Place ice milk slices on half the waffles; top with other halves. Freeze about 30 minutes or until ice milk is set.

Nutrition information: Each serving (2 waffles)

Calories 270	Fat 9 g	**Oat Bran 11 g**
Protein 8 g	polyunsaturated 4 g	Dietary Fiber 3 g
Carbohydrate 43 g	monounsaturated 2 g	Sodium 150 mg
	saturated 2 g	Cholesterol 0 mg

Percentage of calories from fat: 28%
Diabetic exchanges: 2 Starch/Bread; 1½ Fat; 1 Fruit

Cocoa Waffles

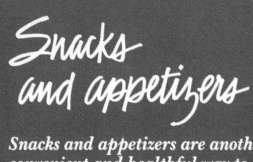

Snacks and appetizers

Snacks and appetizers are another convenient and healthful way to incorporate oat bran into your diet. With these new recipe ideas, snacking can become a welcome part of a proper diet. Try the variety of entertaining, after school and leisure time recipe ideas for between meal treats.

Pictured here are Giant Raisin Oat Cookies and Ginger Cookies. See pages 82 and 83 for recipes.

Giant Raisin Oat Cookies

At last, a rich and chewy cookie that can be part of a fat-modified diet!

¾ cup sugar
⅓ cup light corn syrup
⅓ cup (5⅓ tablespoons)
   margarine, softened
2 egg whites
½ teaspoon grated orange peel
   (optional)

1¼ cups Quaker Oat Bran hot
   cereal, uncooked
1 cup all-purpose flour
1 cup Quaker Oats (quick or old
   fashioned, uncooked)
½ teaspoon baking soda
½ cup raisins

Heat oven to 350°F. Beat sugar, corn syrup and margarine until light and fluffy. Add egg whites and orange peel; beat until well blended. Gradually add combined oat bran, flour, oats and baking soda, mixing well. Stir in raisins. Drop by scant ¼ cups onto ungreased cookie sheet. Gently press into 3-inch circle. Bake 14 to 16 minutes or until light golden brown. Cool 1 minute on cookie sheet; remove to foil. Cool completely. Store tightly covered in freezer or at room temperature.   *Makes 1 dozen*

Tip
To thaw frozen cookies: Unwrap cookies; wrap in paper towel. Microwave at HIGH about 30 seconds per cookie.

Nutrition information: Each serving (1 cookie)

Calories 240	Fat 6 g	**Oat Bran 9 g**
Protein 5 g	polyunsaturated 1 g	Dietary Fiber 2 g
Carbohydrate 42 g	monounsaturated 3 g	Sodium 110 mg
	saturated 1 g	Cholesterol 0 mg

Percentage of calories from fat: 24%
Diabetic exchanges: 1½ Starch/Bread; 1 Fruit; 1 Fat

Ginger Cookies

These crisp cookies are reminiscent of gingersnaps. Great for holidays or a special weekday treat.

¾ cup firmly packed brown sugar
½ cup light corn syrup
½ cup (1 stick) margarine, softened
2 egg whites
3 cups Quaker Oat Bran hot cereal, uncooked

¾ cup all-purpose flour
2 teaspoons ginger
1 teaspoon baking soda
1 teaspoon cinnamon
¼ cup granulated sugar

Heat oven to 350°F. Beat brown sugar, corn syrup and margarine until light and fluffy. Add egg whites; beat until well blended. Gradually add combined oat bran, flour, ginger, baking soda and cinnamon, mixing well. Shape into 1-inch balls; roll in granulated sugar to coat. Place 2 inches apart on ungreased cookie sheet. Gently press balls into 2-inch circles. Bake 11 to 13 minutes or until light golden brown. Cool 1 minute on cookie sheet; remove to foil. Cool completely. Store tightly covered at room temperature. *Makes about 3½ dozen*

Variation: For Yuletide Ginger Cookies, substitute red or green colored sugar for granulated sugar.

Nutrition information: Each serving (2 cookies)

Calories 165	Fat 5 g	**Oat Bran 12 g**
Protein 3 g	polyunsaturated 1 g	Dietary Fiber 2 g
Carbohydrate 26 g	monounsaturated 2 g	Sodium 100 mg
	saturated 1 g	Cholesterol 0 mg

Percentage of calories from fat: 29%
Diabetic exchanges: 1 Starch/Bread; 1 Fat; ½ Fruit

♥   ♥   ♥

Replace up to half the flour in your favorite cookie recipe with oat bran. Depending on the amount of oat bran you wish to incorporate into your daily diet, substitute any percentage of oat bran for the flour up to, but not exceeding, one half.

Shanghai Party Pleasers

Arrange these meatballs on a skewer with crisp vegetables or fresh fruit for an impressive appetizer. Make in the morning, refrigerate, then microwave these meatballs for dinner guests.

1 can (20 oz.) crushed pineapple
    in juice, undrained
¼ cup firmly packed brown
    sugar
2 tablespoons cornstarch
    Dash of ginger
1 cup water
2 tablespoons margarine
1 lb. finely chopped, cooked,
    skinned turkey or chicken

¾ cup Quaker Oat Bran hot
    cereal, uncooked
⅓ cup plain low fat yogurt
⅓ cup finely chopped water
    chestnuts, drained
⅓ cup sliced green onions
2 tablespoons lite soy sauce
1 egg white, slightly beaten
1 teaspoon ginger
½ teaspoon salt (optional)

Drain pineapple, reserving juice. In medium saucepan, combine brown sugar, cornstarch and ginger; mix well. Add combined pineapple juice, water, ¼ cup pineapple and margarine; mix well. Bring to a boil over medium-high heat; reduce heat. Simmer about 1 minute, stirring frequently or until sauce is thickened and clear. Set aside.

Heat oven to 400°F. Lightly spray rack of 13×9-inch baking pan with vegetable oil cooking spray or oil lightly. Combine turkey, oat bran, yogurt, water chestnuts, onions, soy sauce, egg white, ginger, salt and remaining pineapple; mix well. Shape into 1-inch balls. Place on prepared rack. Bake 20 to 25 minutes or until light golden brown. Serve with pineapple sauce. *Makes 2 dozen*

MICROWAVE DIRECTIONS: Drain pineapple, reserving juice. In 2-qt. microwaveable bowl, combine brown sugar, cornstarch and ginger; mix well. Add combined pineapple juice, water, ¼ cup pineapple and margarine; mix well. Microwave at HIGH 5 to 6 minutes or until sauce is thickened and clear, stirring once. Set aside.

Combine turkey, oat bran, yogurt, water chestnuts, onions, soy sauce, egg white, ginger, salt and remaining pineapple; mix well. Shape into 1-inch balls. Place into 11×7-inch microwaveable dish. Cover with waxed paper. Microwave at HIGH 7 to 9 minutes, rearranging twice, or until balls are firm and cooked through. Serve with pineapple sauce.

Nutrition information: Each serving (1/8 of recipe)

Calories 240	Fat 6 g	**Oat Bran 8 g**
Protein 20 g	polyunsaturated 2 g	Dietary Fiber 2 g
Carbohydrate 26 g	monounsaturated 2 g	Sodium 240 mg
	saturated 1 g	Cholesterol 45 mg

Percentage of calories from fat: 24%
Diabetic exchanges: 2½ Lean Meat; 1 Starch/Bread; 1 Fruit

Cocoa Banana Bars

A chocolate lover's delight! Now you can stick to your diet while indulging in this brownie-like treat. Microwave preparation makes this a quick treat throughout the year.

⅔ cup Quaker Oat Bran hot
    cereal, uncooked
⅔ cup all-purpose flour
½ cup granulated sugar
⅓ cup cocoa
½ cup mashed ripe banana
    (about 1 large)
¼ cup liquid vegetable oil
    margarine

3 tablespoons light corn syrup
2 egg whites, slightly beaten
1 teaspoon vanilla
2 teaspoons cocoa
2 teaspoons liquid vegetable oil
    margarine
¼ cup powdered sugar
2 to 2½ teaspoons warm water

Heat oven to 350°F. Lightly spray 8-inch square baking pan with vegetable oil cooking spray or oil lightly. Combine oat bran, flour, granulated sugar and ⅓ cup cocoa. Add combined banana, ¼ cup margarine, corn syrup, egg whites and vanilla; mix well. Pour into prepared pan, spreading evenly. Bake 23 to 25 minutes or until center is set. Cool on wire rack; cut into bars. Store tightly covered.

Top with strawberry halves, if desired. Combine 2 teaspoons cocoa and 2 teaspoons margarine. Stir in powdered sugar and 1 teaspoon water. Gradually add remaining 1 to 1½ teaspoons water to make a medium-thick glaze, mixing well. Drizzle glaze over brownies.   *Makes 9 servings*

MICROWAVE DIRECTIONS: Combine oat bran, flour, granulated sugar and ⅓ cup cocoa. Add combined banana, ¼ cup margarine, corn syrup, egg whites and vanilla; mix well. Pour into 9-inch microwaveable pie plate, spreading evenly. Place in microwave on inverted microwaveable plate. Microwave at HIGH 4 minutes 30 seconds to 5 minutes or until edges are firm to touch, rotating every 2 minutes. To test for doneness, the surface is firm to the touch and the center may appear slightly wet and soft. Cool; cut into wedges. Store tightly covered.

Top with strawberry halves, if desired. Combine 2 teaspoons cocoa and 2 teaspoons margarine. Stir in powdered sugar and 1 teaspoon water. Gradually add remaining 1 to 1½ teaspoons water to make a medium-thick glaze, mixing well. Drizzle glaze over brownies.

Nutrition information: Each serving (⅑ of recipe)

Calories 210	Fat 7 g	Oat Bran 6 g
Protein 4 g	polyunsaturated 4 g	Dietary Fiber 2 g
Carbohydrate 35 g	monounsaturated 1 g	Sodium 60 mg
	saturated 1 g	Cholesterol 0 mg

Percentage of calories from fat: 29%
Diabetic exchanges: 1½ Fat; 1 Starch/Bread; 1 Fruit

Hot Sesame Wafers

Serve these spicy wafers with a yogurt dip. They're great served with salads or low fat cheeses.

½ cup Quaker Oat Bran hot
  cereal, uncooked
½ cup all-purpose flour
½ teaspoon baking powder
¼ teaspoon salt (optional)
¼ teaspoon ground red pepper

2 tablespoons margarine
2 tablespoons light corn syrup
2 tablespoons toasted sesame
  seeds
2 to 3 tablespoons skim milk

Heat oven to 350°F. Combine oat bran, flour, baking powder, salt and red pepper. Add margarine and corn syrup, mixing until mixture resembles coarse crumbs. Stir in sesame seeds. Gradually add milk, mixing just until dough forms a ball. On lightly floured surface, roll out dough to ⅛-inch thickness. Cut with 2-inch biscuit or cookie cutter.* Transfer with spatula to ungreased cookie sheet. Bake 10 to 12 minutes or until firm.

Makes 3 dozen

Note: Serve Hot Sesame Wafers in place of crackers, breadsticks, potato chips, bagel chips or croutons. Serve with soups, salads, dips, juices or stir-fry.

*If dough becomes too stiff, add 1 teaspoon skim milk at a time until of desired consistency.

Nutrition information: Each serving (4 wafers)

Calories 95	Fat 4 g	**Oat Bran 5 g**
Protein 2 g	polyunsaturated 1 g	Dietary Fiber 1 g
Carbohydrate 12 g	monounsaturated 2 g	Sodium 60 mg
	saturated 1 g	Cholesterol 0 mg

Percentage of calories from fat: 39%
Diabetic exchanges: 1 Fat; ½ Starch/Bread

Sugar 'n Spice Topping

Keep a shakerful on hand and sprinkle over fresh fruit or yogurt for a healthy touch of sweetness.

1 cup Quaker Oat Bran hot　　　**½ teaspoon cinnamon**
**　　cereal, uncooked**　　　　　　**¼ teaspoon nutmeg**
¼ cup sugar

Heat oven to 350°F. Place oat bran in ungreased 13×9-inch baking pan. Bake 15 to 17 minutes or until light golden brown, stirring occasionally. Cool; add sugar, cinnamon and nutmeg. Store tightly covered at room temperature. To serve, sprinkle generously on fruit, fruit salads, low fat yogurt, ice milk or pudding. Or, use as a topping for muffins by sprinkling on batter just before baking.　　　　　　*Makes 1¼ cups*

MICROWAVE DIRECTIONS: Place oat bran in 1-qt. microwaveable bowl. Microwave at HIGH 2 to 3 minutes, stirring after every minute. Cool. Add sugar, cinnamon and nutmeg. Store tightly covered at room temperature. To serve, sprinkle generously on fruit, fruit salads, low fat yogurt, ice milk or pudding. Or, use as a topping for muffins by sprinkling on batter just before baking.

Nutrition information: Each serving (1 tablespoon)

Calories 25	Fat 0 g	**Oat Bran 4 g**
Protein 1 g	polyunsaturated 0 g	Dietary Fiber 1 g
Carbohydrate 5 g	monounsaturated 0 g	Sodium 0 mg
	saturated 0 g	Cholesterol 0 mg

Percentage of calories from fat: 13%
Diabetic exchanges: ½ Starch/Bread

Oat Bran
from the Expert ™

Santa Fe Waffles

Try this unique snack with a southwestern accent. Try sprinkling these waffles with part skim mozzarella cheese, broil and serve.

2 medium tomatoes, chopped
½ cup chopped onion
½ cup chopped green bell
    pepper
1 to 2 tablespoons snipped
    fresh cilantro or 1 to
    2 teaspoons cilantro
    leaves, crushed
1 to 2 tablespoons lemon juice
⅛ teaspoon ground red pepper

2 egg whites
1 cup Quaker Oat Bran hot
    cereal, uncooked
1 cup all-purpose flour
2 tablespoons sugar
½ teaspoon baking soda
½ teaspoon baking powder
½ teaspoon salt (optional)
1¼ cups skim milk
3 tablespoons vegetable oil

For salsa, combine tomatoes, onion, green pepper, cilantro, lemon juice and red pepper. Cover; refrigerate at least 1 hour.

Heat waffle iron according to manufacturer's instructions. Beat egg whites until soft peaks form; set aside. Combine oat bran, flour, sugar, baking soda, baking powder and salt; mix well. Whisk milk, oil and ⅔ cup salsa until well blended. Add to dry ingredients, mixing just until moistened. Do not overmix. Fold egg whites into batter. Pour about 1 cup batter onto surface of grid. Close the lid; bake until steam no longer escapes from the sides of the iron and waffles are golden brown. Serve with remaining salsa. *Makes 6 servings*

Variation: For Cheese-Topped Waffles, cut waffles in half diagonally. Top each half with about 1 tablespoon shredded part skim mozzarella cheese. Broil about 1 minute or until cheese is melted. Serve with remaining salsa.

Nutrition information: Each serving (2 waffles)

Calories 250	Fat 8 g	**Oat Bran 14 g**
Protein 8 g	polyunsaturated 4 g	Dietary Fiber 3 g
Carbohydrate 34 g	monounsaturated 2 g	Sodium 150 mg
	saturated 1 g	Cholesterol 0 mg

Percentage of calories from fat: 31%
Diabetic exchanges: 2 Starch/Bread; 1½ Fat; 1 Vegetable

Cocoa Cinnamon Topper

Layer the topping with vanilla yogurt to make a quick parfait or chocolate-flavored treat.

**1 cup Quaker Oat Bran hot
  cereal, uncooked
1 teaspoon grated orange peel
  (optional)**

**¼ cup sugar
1 tablespoon cocoa
½ teaspoon cinnamon**

Heat oven to 350°F. Place oat bran in ungreased 13×9-inch baking pan. Bake 15 to 17 minutes or until light golden brown, stirring occasionally. Stir in orange peel; cool. Add sugar, cocoa and cinnamon. Store tightly covered at room temperature. To serve, sprinkle generously on fruit, fruit salads, low fat yogurt, ice milk or pudding. Or, use as a topping for muffins by sprinkling on batter just before baking.   *Makes 1¼ cups*

MICROWAVE DIRECTIONS: Place oat bran in 1-qt. microwaveable bowl. Microwave at HIGH 2 to 3 minutes, stirring after every minute. Stir in orange peel; cool. Add sugar, cocoa and cinnamon. Store tightly covered at room temperature. To serve, sprinkle generously on fruit, fruit salads, low fat yogurt, ice milk or pudding. Or, use as a topping for muffins by sprinkling on batter just before baking.

Nutrition information: Each serving (1 tablespoon)

Calories 25	Fat 0 g	**Oat Bran 4 g**
Protein 1 g	polyunsaturated 0 g	Dietary Fiber 1 g
Carbohydrate 5 g	monounsaturated 0 g	Sodium 0 mg
	saturated 0 g	Cholesterol 0 mg

Percentage of calories from fat: 13%
Diabetic exchanges: ½ Starch/Bread

Cocoa Cinnamon Topper

Zucchini Spears Olé

Serve these spicy southwestern-style zucchini spears with salsa for an extra punch.

¾ to 1 lb. zucchini (about 2 to 3 small)
¾ cup Quaker Oat Bran hot cereal, uncooked
1 teaspoon chili powder
¾ teaspoon ground cumin

¼ teaspoon ground red pepper
2 egg whites
1½ tablespoons margarine, melted
½ cup homemade salsa (page 90)

Heat oven to 450°F. Lightly spray 15×10-inch baking pan with vegetable oil cooking spray or oil lightly. Cut off ends of zucchini. Cut in half crosswise; slice each piece in half lengthwise, then again in half. In plastic bag, combine oat bran, chili powder, cumin and red pepper. In shallow dish, lightly beat egg whites. Coat zucchini with oat bran mixture; shake off excess. Dip into egg mixture, then coat again with oat bran mixture. Place in prepared pan; lightly brush with margarine. Bake about 20 minutes or until zucchini is crisp-tender. Serve with Homemade Salsa.

Makes 6 servings

Nutrition information: Each serving (3 zucchini spears)

Calories 90	Fat 4 g	**Oat Bran 11 g**
Protein 4 g	polyunsaturated 1 g	Dietary Fiber 2 g
Carbohydrate 10 g	monounsaturated 2 g	Sodium 60 mg
	saturated 0 g	Cholesterol 0 mg

Percentage of calories from fat: 38%
Diabetic exchanges: ½ Starch/Bread; ½ Vegetable; ½ Fat

Oat Bran
from the Expert™

Index